User's Guide to
Christian Belief

To my wonderful son Johnathan

User's Guide to Christian Belief

MARK STIBBE

LION

A Lion Book
an imprint of
Lion Hudson plc
Wilkinson House, Jordan Hill Road,
Oxford OX2 8DR, England
www.lionhudson.com
ISBN 978 0 7459 5231 4

First edition 2007
10 9 8 7 6 5 4 3 2 1 0

Text Acknowledgments
Scripture quotations are taken from the Holy Bible,
New Living Translation, copyright © 1996. Used
by permission of Tyndale House Publishers, Inc.,
Wheaton, Illinois 60189. All rights reserved.

A catalogue record for this book is available
from the British Library

Typeset in 12/13 Lapidary333
Printed and bound in China

Contents

Introduction

One of the most popular TV shows of the last twenty years was called *The X-Files*. It featured two FBI agents called Mulder and Scully whose task was to investigate cases of a paranormal or spiritual nature.

Each episode began with a shot of the basement office of the two agents. In that room hung a poster of a UFO with the words 'I WANT TO BELIEVE' on it. This poster pointed to one of the major themes of the series; indeed, Mulder and Scully play out a continuous contrast in this respect, with Mulder acting the believer and Scully the sceptic. It also pointed to one of the major longings of our times, the longing to believe that we are not alone. As Chris Carter, the producer, said: 'I am a non-religious person in search of a religious experience.'

This book is a simple introduction to what Christians believe. There is a great need for a beginner's guide like this today. Many people are longing to connect with God, but they no longer know what previous generations in most Western nations took for granted – the foundational beliefs of Christianity. Indeed, today there is a great deal of confusion about what Christians believe.

This was born out when a preacher was giving a talk to an audience. He asked one man, 'What do you believe?'

'Well, I believe the same as the church,' the man replied.

'And what does the church believe?'

'Well, they believe the same as me.'

Seeing he was getting nowhere, the preacher said, 'And what is it that you both believe?'

'Well, I suppose the same thing.'

What do Christians believe? Traditionally, Christians have used what are known as 'creeds' as a way of affirming the basic tenets of their faith. A creed (from the Latin *credo*, meaning 'I believe') is simply a statement of faith. The following is known as the 'Apostles' Creed' and is the most popular of the creeds used by Christians in the Western world. It was developed over a period of six centuries (between the second and eighth centuries AD):

We believe in God, the Father almighty,
creator of heaven and earth.

We believe in Jesus Christ, his only Son, our Lord,
who was conceived by the Holy Spirit,
born of the Virgin Mary,
suffered under Pontius Pilate,
was crucified, died, and was buried;
he descended to the dead.
On the third day he rose again;
he ascended into heaven,
he is seated at the right hand of the Father,
and he will come to judge the living and the dead.

> **'The very nature of orthodox Christian faith is that we never come to the end; it begs for more – more discussion, more inquiry, more debate, more questions.'**
> Rob Bell

> We believe in the Holy Spirit,
> the holy catholic Church,
> the communion of saints,
> the forgiveness of sins,
> the resurrection of the body,
> and the life everlasting.

Most of these core beliefs will be covered in this book. It will not be exhaustive, however. I cannot in such a short space describe all the beliefs that Christians hold, nor can I deal with all of the variations in each of the beliefs that I do discuss. This is only an introduction.

My hope is that this volume will stimulate you to go deeper into what Christians believe. If, like the countless fans of *The X-Files*, you want to believe, my prayer is that this book will help you to find faith – specifically faith in the one who is the very heart of Christianity, Jesus Christ.

1 Revelation

Great buildings depend on strong foundations. This is equally true of great systems of faith; they too depend on strong foundations. On what, therefore, do Christians base their beliefs?

There is an intriguing Bible verse that will help answer this question. Deuteronomy 29:29 says:

> There are secret things that belong to the Lord our God, but the revealed things belong to us and our descendants forever, so that we may obey these words of the law.

Here the Bible makes reference to things that are concealed and things that are revealed. God has kept certain things secret; they remain known to him alone and are a mystery to humanity. At the same time, God has chosen to reveal many things too. These are

no longer a mystery and we – and those who come after us – can be certain about them.

The conclusion to be drawn from this is that there are some areas where there is ambiguity and others where there is certainty. We may have to embrace ambiguity where God has concealed his ways. But we can embrace certainty where he has revealed his ways. Those who are Christians don't know all the answers but they do know some. And the answers they do know, they can be confident about. These answers can form a firm foundation for their beliefs.

The key word in all of this is 'revelation'. If God had not chosen to reveal himself, Christians would have nothing to believe in the first place. Put another way, Christians would not know about God if God had not chosen to make himself known. Before anything else, therefore, we must look at how God has revealed himself.

General revelation

According to the Bible, there are two ways in which God has chosen to reveal himself. The first is often referred to as 'general revelation'. General revelation is available to all people. It is revelation of a non-verbal kind. In other words, it does not involve God speaking to human beings in words.

General revelation comes in three main ways.

First of all, it comes through nature. I wonder if you have ever found yourself in a context of unusual natural beauty and felt a profound sense of joy or wonder, almost worship. If you have, this would not by any means be unusual. Many people see God's hand in nature – whether they are Christians or not.

The Bible teaches that God reveals himself in and through the beauty and intricacy of the cosmos. In Psalm 19:1–4 the songwriter describes how God reveals himself non-verbally through his creation:

'The world is mud-luscious and puddle-wonderful.'

e.e. cummings

The heavens tell of the glory of God.
The skies display his marvellous craftsmanship.
Day after day they continue to speak;
night after night they make him known.
They speak without a sound or a word;
their voice is silent in the skies;
yet their message has gone out to all the earth,
and their words to all the world.

Another famous passage on this subject is found in Romans
1:20, where the apostle Paul writes:

From the time the world was created, people have seen the earth and sky
and all that God made. They can clearly see his invisible qualities – his
eternal power and divine nature. So they have no excuse whatsoever for
not knowing God.

In Daniel Defoe's famous novel *Robinson Crusoe*, it was a

footprint in the sand that revealed to the hero that he was not alone. Similarly, nature is covered in footprints that indicate that we are not alone in this universe, that there is a Creator. Many have testified to this over the centuries. For instance, on 1 November 1988, John Glenn made the following comment from the Discovery Space Shuttle: 'I don't think you can be up here and look out the window as I did the first day and see the earth from this vantage point, to look out at this kind of creation and not believe in God.' Such comments have been common through the ages.

Nature is one source of general revelation about God. At the same time it is limited. Nature may lead people to sense the existence of a Creator but it does not show them how to enter into a relationship with God.

A second way in which general revelation comes is through conscience, through humanity's innate sense of right and wrong. Have you ever had the feeling that you just knew in your heart that something you were about to do was morally wrong? Many people have had precisely this experience of their conscience pointing to an objective moral law.

The classic biblical statement about this can be found in what the apostle Paul says in Romans 2:14–15.

'Most of us follow our conscience as we follow a wheelbarrow. We push it in front of us in the direction we want to go.'

Billy Graham

Even when Gentiles, who do not have God's written law, instinctively follow what the law says, they show that in their hearts they know right from wrong. They demonstrate that God's law is written within them, for their own consciences either accuse them or tell them they are doing what is right.

Immanuel Kant once said, 'Two things continue to fill the mind with ever increasing awe and admiration: the starry heavens above and the moral law within.' Conscience is an extremely important guide to what is right and what is wrong. It is the inner voice that tells people that someone may be looking. It is what hurts when everything else feels so good. It is the moral law within.

At the same time conscience is not a sufficient guide for

showing how to enter into a relationship with God. Conscience tells people to do what's right but it does not ultimately reveal what right and wrong are, or where they come from. For that people need something – or someone – greater than conscience.

The third way in which general revelation comes is through history. History consistently demonstrates the truth of Proverbs 14:34 – 'Godliness exalts a nation, but sin is a disgrace to any people.' Put another way, history reveals time and time again that in the long run the godly prosper and the wicked do not. Obedience to God's law in society ultimately brings blessings. Disobedience results in curses. This truth is played out throughout history.

However, history – like nature and conscience – is a very limited source of revelation about God. This is for two reasons; first of all, people are not usually very smart when it comes to learning from history. Hegel puts it bluntly, 'What experience and history teach is this – that people and governments never have learned anything from history, or acted on principles deduced from it.' The second reason is that history in and of itself does not explain how humans can relate to God.

> **'History repeats itself. It has to. No one listens.'**
>
> Steve Turner

General revelation is not enough

General revelation is not enough if people are going to connect with the living God. God says in Isaiah 55:8–9,

> *'My thoughts are completely different from yours,' says the Lord. 'And my ways are far beyond anything you could imagine. For just as the heavens are higher than the earth, so are my ways higher than your ways and my thoughts higher than your thoughts.'*

Even with the help of nature, conscience and history, the human mind is too finite and fallible to know God personally. The apostle Paul describes how fallible the human mind is in Ephesians 4:18–19.

Their closed minds are full of darkness; they are far away from the life of God because they have shut their minds and hardened their hearts against him. They don't care anymore about right and wrong, and they have given themselves over to immoral ways. Their lives are filled with all kinds of impurity and greed.

What the Bible calls 'sin' (see Chapter 4) has all but obliterated the knowledge of God. That is why what is known as 'natural theology' is insufficient. Natural theology is the attempt to know and understand God without reference to the Bible and with reference only to nature, conscience and history. The great problem with this is the finite nature of human thinking. How

could a limited human mind ever comprehend the vast and infinite nature of God? Even the greatest thinkers recognize their limitations here. Sir Isaac Newton once memorably remarked in relation to his own scientific discoveries, 'I appear to have been like a boy playing upon the seashore and diverting myself and then finding a smoother pebble or prettier shell than ordinary, while the great ocean of truth lay before me undiscovered.'

In the final analysis the human mind is limited by its finitude and perverted by its rejection of God. Natural theology is of some value but it will not be sufficient to lead a person into a relationship with the living God. It is quite simply not enough.

Special revelation

Christians believe that God has provided not only general revelation of himself but also a second kind of revelation known as 'special revelation'. This is second not in importance but in time. Special revelation occurs after general revelation has begun.

The special revelation of God is communicated primarily in the pages of the Bible. In the Old and New Testaments, God reveals how we can begin an eternal friendship with him. If general revelation points to God the Creator, special revelation points to God the Redeemer.

There are a number of things to note about special revelation. First of all, it is 'particular'. In other words, God has chosen to reveal himself through a particular people. God began the process of special revelation through his chosen people, Israel. As God says to Abraham in Genesis 12:1–3:

> Then the Lord told Abram, 'Leave your country, your relatives, and your father's house, and go to the land that I will show you. I will cause you to become the father of a great nation. I will bless you and make you famous, and I will make you a blessing to others. I will bless those who bless you and curse those who curse you. All the families of the earth will be blessed through you.'

'The Bible is more epic in its scope than *The Lord of the Rings*, has more adventure than *Indiana Jones*, more romance than *Casablanca* and in terms of popularity leaves the *Star Wars* movies trailing in its wake.'

Mark Stibbe

God's plan from the beginning was to reveal himself to a particular people and through that people to reveal himself to all peoples. God spoke to Israel. Israel was to speak to the world.

The second thing to say is that special revelation is 'progressive'. The Bible tells the unfolding story of God's actions in history. As we read more and more about what God has said and done, we learn more and more about his nature. This does not mean that the Bible begins with a false revelation of God and then proceeds to a true one. Rather it means that the Bible begins with a partial revelation of God and then, in Jesus, moves on to a complete one. As the writer to the Hebrews puts it:

> Long ago God spoke many times and in many ways to our ancestors through the prophets. But now in these final days, he has spoken to us through his Son.
>
> Hebrews 1:2

The third thing to note is that special revelation is 'proclaimed'. Special revelation comes with *words*, through proclaimed divine speech. We have already seen how general revelation is non-verbal in form. Psalm 19 tells us that the heavens tell of the glory of God but they do so in words that are silent. In special revelation, the picture is altogether different. Now God speaks. He uses human language to disclose himself. In the quotation from Hebrews above we should note the claim that 'God spoke' through the prophets and has now 'spoken to us through his Son'. God communicates verbally through the prophets in the Old Testament; he communicates verbally through Jesus and the apostles in the New Testament.

The fourth thing to say is that special revelation is 'perfected' revelation. The climax of God's personal revelation to humanity

Christian understandings of the Bible	
Roman Catholic	Authoritative revelation comes from the Bible (including 'the Apocrypha') and from church tradition and teaching
Evangelical	Authoritative revelation comes from the Bible alone (*sola scriptura*, in Latin) – which is God's Word, free from error
Orthodox	Authoritative revelation comes from the Bible and from wider church tradition, which includes a number of unwritten beliefs
Liberal	The Bible is open to human interpretation in the light of historical and literary context and cannot be treated as an infallible record. Its historical reliability and miraculous elements are therefore questioned
Existential	The Bible is a book of myths that need stripping of their supernatural elements so that they can be used as a source of guidance and encounter
Liberation	The Bible is a book of stories about emancipation which give meaning and hope to those who need to experience freedom today

is Jesus Christ. Through his Son, God reveals himself in a unique and final way. As John 1:17–18 puts it:

> *For the law was given through Moses; God's unfailing love and faithfulness*
> *came through Jesus Christ. No one has ever seen God. But his only Son,*
> *who is himself God, is near to the Father's heart; he has told us about*
> *him.*

Many Christians believe that we do not need any further revelation of God. If we want to know God, we have everything we need in the Bible, thanks to God's revelation of himself in Jesus Christ and through his apostles. This view is known as 'the sufficiency of Scripture'. The best definition I have read of the sufficiency of the Bible is by the Protestant theologian Wayne Grudem, who says, 'The sufficiency of Scripture means that Scripture contained all the words of God he intended his people to have at each stage of redemptive history, and that it now contains all the words of God we need for salvation.'

The fifth thing to say is that special revelation is 'powerful'. It achieves what general revelation cannot. While general revelation can help us to know God as Creator, only special revelation can enable us to know God as Father. Without the self-disclosure of God in the Bible we would not have come to know what God is really like. And we certainly couldn't have begun a relationship of trust with the living God. Special revelation is powerful. As the apostle Paul says:

> *Now God has shown us a different way of being right in his sight — not by*
> *obeying the law but by the way promised in the Scriptures long ago. We*
> *are made right in God's sight when we trust in Jesus Christ to take away*
> *our sins. And we all can be saved in this same way, no matter who we are*
> *or what we have done.*
> Romans 3:21–22

The final thing to say is that special revelation is 'personal'. General revelation through nature, conscience and history may help us to know God, but not in a personal way. Only through special revelation can we know God personally. God's desire

has always been for an intimate and loving relationship with human beings. He has pursued us relentlessly in love, not so that we may study him as detached observers, but so that we may adore him as passionate worshippers.

Right from the beginning, God has wanted human beings to know him personally. Listen to these very affectionate words from one of the earliest books in the Old Testament:

> 'The Lord did not choose you and lavish his love on you because you were larger or greater than other nations, for you were the smallest of all nations! It was simply because the Lord loves you, and because he was keeping the oath he had sworn to your ancestors.'
> Deuteronomy 7:7–8

By revealing himself once and for all in his Son, God has made a personal knowledge of himself a possibility for all people.

We can't do without the Bible

Christians believe that we cannot do without the Bible if we are to have right beliefs. God's special revelation of himself has been written down and recorded for all time in the pages of the Holy Bible. We accordingly need the Bible. It is God's Word to humanity. If we want to know what God wants us to believe, then we must be avid students of his book.

I cannot give a full description of the Bible, its complexity and its importance at this point, but there are two things that we need to note here. The first concerns the authority of the Bible.

The Bible has a unique authority when it comes to speaking about God. This includes the Old Testament. The Old Testament writers declared 3,808 times that they were writing God's Word. Jesus quoted the Old Testament 180 times in his teaching. This clearly shows that the Old as well as the New Testament has unique authority. As we read in Hebrews 4:12:

> For the word of God is full of living power. It is sharper than the sharpest knife, cutting deep into our innermost thoughts and desires. It exposes us for what we really are.

God's Word has great authority because its author is God! As British Prime Minister William Gladstone (1809–98) said, 'The Bible is stamped with a speciality of origin and an immeasurable distance separates it from all competitors.'

The second issue concerns the inspiration of the Bible. It never ceases to amaze me that the Bible was written in three different languages – Hebrew, Aramaic and Greek; that it was written by nearly forty different human authors; that these human authors wrote over a period of 1,500 years; that these authors came from a range of social backgrounds (kings, priests, prophets, shepherds, fishermen, a tax collector, a physician); that they wrote from different parts of the world (such as Israel, Egypt, Rome, Babylon, Ephesus, Greece, Syria, Assyria); that they wrote on hundreds of topics, many of which were highly controversial – and yet, in spite of this great diversity, the Bible is a unified book.

The reason for this is that the Bible is inspired throughout by God's Spirit, whom Christians call the 'Holy Spirit' (see Chapter 8). While there are many different authors, contexts and genres in the Bible, there is also a Spirit-inspired unity from the beginning of Genesis to the end of Revelation. As Paul wrote in his second letter to Timothy:

> *All Scripture is inspired by God and is useful to teach us what is true and to make us realize what is wrong in our lives. It straightens us out and teaches us to do what is right. It is God's way of preparing us in every way, fully equipped for every good thing God wants us to do.*
> 2 Timothy 3:16–17

Christians believe that the Bible contains God's special revelation of himself. They also believe that the Bible is inspired by the Holy Spirit and that we need his help if we are properly to understand it. In other words, we need to allow the same Spirit who inspired the Scriptures in their composition to inspire us in their interpretation.

For Christians the Bible is essential for understanding what to believe. And yet the Bible is far more than just a book of beliefs. The Bible tells the big story of human history, from creation to recreation. Human beings are actors in that story. As readers, we therefore cannot be detached as we interpret it. As the South African theologian Kwame Bediako beautifully puts it:

> Scripture is the living testimony to what God has done and continues to do, and we are part of that testimony. The characters in Scripture are both our contemporaries and our ancestors. Their triumphs and failures help us understand our own journey of faith (Romans 11:18). Scripture is not something we only believe in, it is something we share in.

The Bible is therefore the foundation for all that Christians believe. In the Bible, God himself has disclosed the story of his actions from the beginning of the universe to the end of time. We are actors in this great, overarching story. We find our moorings in the cosmos once we become reconnected to the God of the Bible. The Bible is therefore at the heart of Christian belief.

2 God

Trying to explain God is a little bit like trying to control a tornado. Just as a tornado won't be tied down, so God will not be limited by human attempts to define him. He is simply too big for that. As the early church preacher John Chrysostom once wrote, 'A comprehended God is no God.'

While this is true, there are certain things that Christians can say about God because he has chosen to reveal them. This revelation – as we saw in the last chapter – has come through the written Word of God (the Bible) and through God's Word in human form (Jesus Christ). What Christians believe about God is therefore not the product of humans trying to ascend to an understanding of God through reason. It is the result of God descending to where we are and revealing himself to us. As the nineteenth-century historian Thomas Arnold once said, 'The distinction between Christianity and other systems of religion consists largely in this, that in these others people are found seeking after God, while Christianity is God seeking after people.'

With that in mind we now embark on a brief discussion of four Christian beliefs: the existence of God, the attributes of God, the names of God and, finally, what may be referred to as the triunity of God (God as 'Three-in-One').

The existence of God

Christians believe that God exists, simple as that! How they come to that conclusion is however a more complicated matter. There are essentially two ways in which a Christian comes to believe that God exists. The first is by reason.

Great Christian thinkers over the centuries have come up with many different arguments for the existence of God. The four that continue to be most popular are the cosmological

argument, the teleological argument, the experiential argument and the moral argument.

The cosmological argument begins with the cosmos. Observing change in the universe, the cosmologist notes that a thing cannot change itself. Some agent is required. Go back far enough and there must be some Changer at the start of the process. This first cause of change is not changed by anything and therefore must be God.

Similar reasoning is applied to existence. A being exists because something that already exists brings it into existence. Everything must therefore ultimately owe its existence to something or someone that existed before them. This position, in simple terms, runs like this:

Everything in the cosmos depends on something else for its existence.

What is true of the parts of the cosmos is true of the whole cosmos.

The cosmos therefore depends on something else for its existence.

The cosmos must therefore depend on God as long as it exists.

The cosmological argument not only looks at change and existence, it also depends on the idea of 'cause and effect'. Every effect has a cause. There cannot be an infinite regress of finite causes. Therefore there must be an uncaused Causer of effects, and that must be God.

Whichever form it takes (change, existence, cause or other concepts, such as degrees), the cosmological viewpoint – often associated with medieval theologian Thomas Aquinas (c. 1225–74) – continues to be popular. More recently it has been refined into what is known as the *kalam* argument put forward by William Craig Lane in his book *The Existence of God and the Origins of the Universe*.

A second rational case for the existence of God is known as the teleological argument. The word 'teleology' comes from the Greek words *teleios* (meaning 'end') and *logos* (meaning 'speech'). Teleology is accordingly 'speaking about the end, the purpose, or the design of something'.

The teleological position is also known as the argument from design. There is order and design in the universe and this cannot be attributed to the objects themselves. This is especially true of inanimate objects. Therefore design points to a Designer. The intelligent being who designed everything is God.

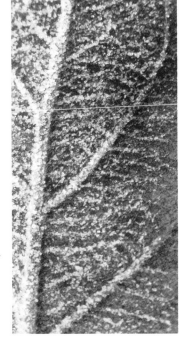

The eighteenth-century English philosopher William Paley wrote a famous book in 1802 called *Natural Theology*. In it he claimed that a person who discovered a stone in a field would not ask how that stone came to be there. However, the same person discovering a watch in a field would certainly ask how it came to be there. The reason why the person would ask this about a watch and not a stone is because a watch exhibits the appearance of design while a stone doesn't. The inference that person would draw from such an appearance of design is that the watch has a designer or creator. This is true of the cosmos as a whole; it exhibits the appearance of design and therefore must have a designer or creator. While there have been counter-arguments to this (not least that creation exhibits chaos and suffering), the teleological argument continues to prove popular. Today there is a great deal of discussion about 'intelligent design' and whether or not it should be taught alongside evolutionary theory in schools.

> 'We had the sky, up there, all speckled with stars, and we used to lay on our backs and look up at them, and discuss whether they was made, or only just happened.'
>
> Mark Twain, *Huckleberry Finn*

The third argument I call the experiential viewpoint. People experience spiritual hunger. Just as physical hunger indicates the existence of food so spiritual hunger indicates the existence of God. As C. S. Lewis once said, 'If I find in myself a desire which no experience in this world can satisfy, the most probable explanation is that I was made for another world.' The pervasiveness of this spiritual longing, along with the widespread evidence for the innate idea and the actual experience of God, suggests the existence of something or someone to which these things are directed.

The fourth and final position is the argument from morality, often associated with Immanuel Kant (1724–1804). Kant argued that every human being has an innate moral impulse. We all have a sense of what we ought to do and what we ought not to do. Where does this pressure come from? Kant argued that it comes from a supreme being who supports the moral order of the universe and who ultimately rewards good and punishes evil.

These four arguments – along with others – represent the rational basis for the existence of God. However, Christians recognize that reason alone can only get a person so far. They do not provide a firm assurance that God exists or that God is personal and loving. All they do is suggest the probability of the existence of God, or a god, or even gods. This is why Christians base their belief about the existence of God not primarily on reason but on revelation. By 'revelation' I mean what in the last chapter I referred to as 'special revelation' – God's revelation of himself in and through his Word. Christians believe in God's existence not so much because they have reasoned their way to that conclusion but because God has revealed himself as living

Arguments for the existence of God	
Cosmological argument	Points to change, existence and cause, and argues for a first cause or Causer
Teleological argument	Points to the design of the universe indicating the existence of a Designer or Creator
Experiential argument	Points to spiritual hunger, suggesting there is a God who can satisfy this longing
Moral argument	Points to man's sense of 'ought', suggesting the existence of a supreme moral being

and real. This doesn't mean that reason is unimportant; it simply means that revelation precedes reason. Put another way, I do not understand in order to believe; I believe in order that I may understand.

The attributes of God

It is really fair to say that the Bible assumes the existence of God rather than argues for it. Right from the very first verses of the book of Genesis, God speaks, and he acts in the world. The Bible is not a book that promotes atheism – the view that God did not create the world and does not control the world. Nor is it a book that promotes deism – the view that God created the world but does not control it. The Bible at every point promotes theism – the view that God created the world and controls the world.

The Bible says many magnificent things about the nature of God. These attributes have often been divided into two categories – those that are incommunicable and those that are communicable. Incommunicable attributes are those that are God's alone and are not shared with us. Communicable attributes are those that belong to God but which he shares with us.

No treatment of these attributes can be final and exhaustive,

'I believe in God like I believe in the sun rise; not because I can see it but because I can see all that it touches.'

C. S. Lewis

25

but the following are some examples from Scripture of God's incommunicable attributes.

- Infinity – God is without beginning and end (Psalm 90:2)

- Independence – God is self-existent and independent from his creation (Psalm 115:3)

- Immutability – God is unchanging (James 1:17)

- Omniscience – God knows all things (Psalm 139:1–4)

- Omnipresence – God is present everywhere (Psalm 139:7–12)

- Omnipotence – God is all-powerful (Matthew 19:26; Revelation 19:6)

These are some examples from Scripture of God's communicable attributes:

- Holiness – God is set apart from all sin (1 Peter 1:16)

- Patience – God is long suffering and persistent (2 Peter 3:9)

- Goodness – God is a benevolent being (Exodus 33:19; Psalm 145:9)

- Grace – God gives undeserved favour to the needy (Exodus 34:6)

- Mercy – God is tender-hearted towards the needy (Exodus 3:6)

- Justice – God shows perfect equity and fairness (Romans 2:11)

- Faithfulness – God is true to his promises (Numbers 23:19)

- Sovereignty – God is supreme ruler over all (Ephesians 1:21)

And above all:

- Love – God seeks our good at his own personal cost (John 3:16)

The nature of God	
Main description	God is a Spirit
Incommunicable attributes	Infinite Eternal Unchangeable
Communicable attributes	Being Wisdom Power Holiness Justice Goodness Truth

It is interesting to note that what is known as the Westminster Shorter Catechism offers the following definition of God: 'God is a Spirit, infinite, eternal and unchangeable in His being, wisdom, power, holiness, justice, goodness and truth.' Here we see both incommunicable attributes (such as infiniteness) and communicable attributes (such as holiness).

Such are some of the attributes of God. They cannot possibly say everything that could be said about God. As the poet Tennyson says in his poem 'In Memoriam':

Our little systems have their day,
They have their day and cease to be:
They are but broken lights of Thee,
And Thou, O Lord, art more than they.

Nevertheless, these attributes are revealed by God in the Bible rather than deduced by man through reason. As such they have great value in both our knowledge of God and our worship of him.

The names of God

If Christians believe in the existence and the attributes of God, they also believe in the names of God. There are many names revealed in the Bible. We will just mention a few here.

The names of God in the Bible have been communicated to us by God, not made up by man. These names are far more than just designations; they are revelations of God's character. So, for example, in the Old Testament there are Hebrew names for God that use the word *El,* meaning 'strength' and translated 'God'. These include: *El Elyon,* meaning 'God Most High' (Genesis 14:18–22); *El Shaddai*, meaning 'God Almighty' (Genesis 17:1); and *El Olam*, meaning 'Everlasting God' (Genesis 21:23). These are just some of what are referred to as the 'Elohistic' names for God (from the word *El*).

Then there are what are known as 'Jehovah' names. These have the word Yahweh or Jehovah in front of them. When God revealed his name to Moses, he said, 'I am what I am', pointing to his eternal or continuing existence (Exodus 3:13–15). The phrase 'I am what I am' is very hard to translate but it contains the Hebrew verb *hayah*, meaning 'to be'. I like to translate Yahweh or Jehovah as 'Always'. The box opposite lists some of the Jehovah names for God in the Old Testament.

There are other names in the Old Testament for God, such as *Adonai* ('Lord'). But I want briefly to mention the biblical name for God that is regarded by many as the most important one of all – namely 'Father'.

From time to time in the Old Testament there are references to God as a loving Father (Isaiah 63:16). But it is really in Jesus that this image of God comes to the fore. When Jesus addressed God in prayer or worship he used the Aramaic word *Abba*, which means 'Daddy'. When he encouraged his followers to pray he asked them to begin with the words 'Our Father'. Everywhere you look in the New Testament, God is revealed time and time again as Father. To be sure, there are other things said about God; that he is Judge, for example. But the premier name for God revealed by Jesus is Father. If Jesus hadn't disclosed this name, we would never have known it or used it. No other religion provides us with this extraordinary insight. Only Jesus shows us that the one who created the heavens and the earth is the Father we've been waiting for. As Jesus said, 'I am the way, the truth, and the life; no one can come to *the Father* except through me' (John 14:6). The Son is the only one who reveals the Father. 'Father' is

Biblical names for God

Name	Meaning	Passage
Jehovah Mekaddesh	Always our Sanctifier	Leviticus 20:8
Jehovah Tsidkenu	Always our Righteousness	Jeremiah 23:6
Jehovah Jireh	Always our Provider	Genesis 22:13–14
Jehovah Shalom	Always our Peace	Judges 6:22–24
Jehovah Shammah	Always There	Ezekiel 48:35
Jehovah Rapha	Always our Healer	Exodus 15:22–26
Jehovah Ra'ah	Always our Shepherd	Psalm 23:1
Jehovah Nissi	Always our Banner	Exodus 17:15

the greatest of all the Christian names for God. That is why the Apostles' Creed begins, 'We believe in God, *the Father* Almighty'.

The triunity of God

In speaking of the Father and the Son we are moving already to the fourth and perhaps most distinctive belief that a Christian holds about God – and that is the *triunity* of God.

The word 'triunity' points to the fact that in Christianity God is believed to be Three-in-One and One-in-Three. Christians believe that there is only one God. They also believe that God has revealed himself in Scripture as three persons – Father, Son and Holy Spirit. They finally believe that these three persons are one and the same God.

In Chapter 1 we mentioned the progressive nature of God's special revelation in the Bible. Here is an example of that. In the Old Testament there are hints that there is more than one person in God. Take the following verse as an example:

Then God said, 'Let us make people in our image, to be like ourselves. They will be masters over all life – the fish in the sea, the birds in the sky, and all the livestock, wild animals, and small animals.'
Genesis 1:26

Here God says, 'Let *us* make people in *our* image.' Who is he speaking to? Many Christians believe that this is a very early indication that God is Three-in-One and that the Father is speaking to the Son and to the Spirit. Then there is the story about Abraham at the oak grove at Mamre (Genesis 18). He is visited by three mysterious men, whom Abraham addresses as 'Lord'. Some Christians believe that the visitors were angels, but many Christians believe that Abraham is receiving a revelation of God as Triune.

While this revelation is only implicit in the Old Testament it becomes more explicit in the New Testament. As the old saying goes, 'The Old Testament is the New concealed; the New Testament is the Old revealed.' While the word 'Trinity' is never used in the New Testament, the New Testament Scriptures show a progression towards clearer proofs. The scope of God's plan of salvation involves the Father sending the Son and then the Son sending the Spirit. Jesus' final words to his disciples – known as the Great Commission – point to the triunity of God:

> *Therefore, go and make disciples of all the nations, baptizing them in the name of the Father and the Son and the Holy Spirit.*
> Matthew 28:19

Paul's blessing at the end of 2 Corinthians 13 points to the same:

> *May the grace of our Lord Jesus Christ, the love of God, and the fellowship of the Holy Spirit be with you all.*

The New Testament therefore speaks about three persons in the Godhead. The first is the Father. He is the Creator of all things, the Father of Israel, the Father of Jesus, and the Father of all believers. This indicates that the Father is the first person of the Trinity.

Then there is the Son. Jesus is the Son, or the Son of God. He is the second person of the Trinity. He is the One and Only Son of God by nature. Through the Son, the Father creates the universe. Through the Son, the Father redeems humanity.

Then there is the Holy Spirit. Like the Father and the Son, the Spirit is referred to as a person. In John 14:16 Jesus refers to the Spirit with the pronoun 'he', not 'it' (see Chapter 8). The Spirit is therefore not an impersonal force but the third person of the Trinity.

Now the Bible does not present these three persons as three separate individuals, as three gods or three disguises. Rather, the New Testament indicates (and later Christian theology elucidates) that there are three persons in the Godhead and that these three are the one true God, the same in being, even though they can be distinguished by their personal properties.

It is very difficult to explain in simple language how exactly three can be one and one can be three. St Patrick used to use a shamrock to illustrate the Trinity. He would hold up a shamrock to the pagans and ask if he was holding one leaf or three. But this illustration has its difficulties too. No analogy seems ultimately to give a satisfactory explanation of how three persons can be one and the same being. As John Wesley once remarked, 'Tell me how it is that in this room there are three candles and but one light; and I will explain to you the mode of the divine existence.'

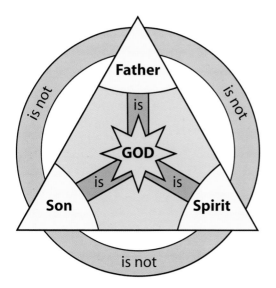

This diagram helps to give a clearer picture of what Christians believe when they speak about the Trinity, even if it doesn't ultimately explain it. If you look at the diagram you will see that the Father, the Son and the Spirit are all God (see the centre). At the same time, the Father is not the same as the Son or the Spirit, the Son is not the same as the Spirit or the Father, and the Spirit is not the same as the Son or the Father (see the outer circle).

But even with the help of a diagram like this, there is still a limit to what human language can describe. How can God be both 'he' and 'they'? How can God be one being and yet at the same time have three personal centres of rational awareness? And how do these three persons relate co-equally when the Bible also tells us that the Son obeys the Father (John 5:30)?

The belief in the triunity of God is ultimately a mystery and continues to provoke debate. Other aspects of God's nature have also stimulated great amounts of discussion in recent years.

The idea of God's 'impassibility' has been hotly debated. Is God incapable of experiencing suffering, as this word literally denotes? Or has Christ's experience of being tortured and killed been taken up into the Godhead, enabling us to speak – as Martin Luther did – of 'the Crucified God'?

God's providence is also a controversial issue. Does God cause everything to occur, right down to the finest detail? Some Christians (following John Calvin) believe that God wills everything to happen; this view is known as absolute sovereignty. Others (following Jacob Arminius) believe that God foresees everything but that he does not necessarily cause all of those things to happen. Still others believe in 'open theism', arguing that God foreordains some things but also leaves a lot open, so that human beings have the ability to create their futures, good or bad.

Another area of dispute is the belief that God is transcendent and immanent. Process theology has tended to deny that God is the all-powerful ruler over creation. Instead, it claims that God contains the universe and that the universe is in a constant process of change. This view has not found its way into mainstream theology because it denies what the Bible clearly reveals: that God is both transcendent and immanent; he is both the Most High and the Most Nigh.

When it comes to speaking about God, while there is a lot of certainty, there is also mystery. As the American pastor Rob Bell puts it, 'The moment God is figured out with nice neat lines and definitions, we are no longer dealing with God. We are dealing with somebody we made up. And if we made him up, then we are in control.' Perhaps the best thing to do is to agree with the words of Psalm 139:6:

> *Such knowledge is too wonderful for me,*
> *too great for me to know!*

> **'I would rather live my life as if there is a God and die to find out there isn't, than live my life as if there isn't and die to find out there is.'**
>
> Albert Camus

3 Creation

A recent article in a national newspaper revealed some interesting statistics on what students in the UK believe about the origins of the universe. More than 30 per cent said they believed in 'intelligent design' and 'creationism' (that the design visible in the world points to it being created by God). In stark contrast, the percentage of students who believe in the theory of evolution was said to be decreasing.

> 'It's supposed to be a secular society but I look around: everybody's religious... It's not that far below the surface. We've gone two hundred years since the Enlightenment, but science is starting to bow again.'
>
> Bono, U2

Did the world come about by chance? Or did God create the world?

In this chapter we will look at seven Christian beliefs about the creation of the universe.

The universe was created from nothing

As we saw in Chapter 1, the Bible is God's special revelation of himself to human beings. It begins with the most magnificent description of the creation of the world. In Genesis 1:1–5 we read:

> In the beginning God created the heavens and the earth. The earth was empty, a formless mass cloaked in darkness. And the Spirit of God was hovering over its surface. Then God said, 'Let there be light,' and there was light. And God saw that it was good. Then he separated the light from the darkness. God called the light 'day' and the darkness 'night'. Together these made up one day.

The Bible starts with the phrase 'In the beginning'. In other words, there was a point in time when the universe began. The Bible does not teach that the universe has always existed, or that matter is eternal. The ancient Greek notion that the universe is

infinite is not something taught in Scripture. The words 'In the beginning' signify a definite start to the universe. Before that moment, there was nothing.

According to the Bible God created all things from nothing, a belief sometimes referred to by the Latin phrase *creatio ex nihilo*. It is interesting to note that many scientists agree with this idea of creation out of nothing. They point to their belief that the universe is expanding, which indicates that there must have been a fixed point from which the universe exploded. They talk about the 'singularity' or 'big bang' – an explosion in space–time when the entire physical universe burst forth from a single point of density.

What many scientists are saying is this: there was a transcendent, cosmic beginning to the universe, and the universe has been continually expanding at extraordinary speed from that fixed point.

Before we move to the next belief about creation, it may not be insignificant that the Bible confirms both of these discoveries. In Isaiah 42:5 the prophet declares, 'God, the Lord, created the heavens and *stretched them out.*'

Two things are said here: first that the universe began as a result of God's creative work. This means that if a singularity did occur (and there is still debate about that) it did not occur randomly. There was a Creator responsible for that extraordinary transition from nothing to something.

Secondly, the verse says that God stretched out the heavens. A number of Bible verses talk about the heavens being 'stretched out', for example, Job 9:8; Psalm 104:2; and Isaiah 40:22. The verb used clearly denotes expansion. Sometimes the verb used is in the past tense, to describe something that happened. Sometimes it is used in the present tense, to indicate a process that is still taking place. This is exactly what many scientists – especially astrophysicists – have observed.

> 'God sits enthroned above the circle of the earth, and its people are like grasshoppers. He stretches out the heavens like a canopy, and spreads them out like a tent to live in...'
>
> Isaiah 40:22

This means the Bible taught that the universe had a beginning from nothing well before the discovery of the singularity. It also means that the Bible taught that the universe was expanding well before the discovery of relativity. Alan Sandage, winner of the Crawford prize in astronomy, has concluded this: 'I find it quite improbable that such order came out of chaos. There has to be some organizing principle. God to me is a mystery but is the explanation for the miracle of existence, why there is something instead of nothing.'

The universe was created by God

The opening verse of the book of Genesis indicates this second belief. Here we learn that 'God created'. The Hebrew verb 'create' is *bara*, which tends to be used of God in the Old Testament. It means 'to bring something previously non-existent into existence'. Since God alone can create something out of nothing, it follows that the word *bara* should be reserved for him.

This word *bara* or 'create' is used three times in the first chapter of Genesis. It is used in verse 1 for God creating the heavens and the earth. It is used in verse 21 for God creating the sea creatures and every sort of fish and every sort of bird. Finally it is used in verse 27 for God creating human beings in his own image. In all three instances this verb has God as its subject.

What this shows is that the creation of the heavens and the earth, the creation of the sea creatures and birds, and the creation of human beings were all the result of the creative action of God. They were not chance events. In every case (and indeed in every other case mentioned in Genesis 1), God did something totally new. The universe therefore did not come about through the fortuitous outcome of thousands of linked happenings. It was the result of God's creative activity.

More than that, a Christian will want to add that the universe was created by the Triune God (see Chapter 2). From a Christian perspective, the following verses are very significant:

In the beginning God created the heavens and the earth.
Genesis 1:1

The earth was empty, a formless mass cloaked in darkness. And the Spirit of God was hovering over its surface.
Genesis 1:2

Then God said, 'Let there be light,'...
Genesis 1:3

From the early church onwards, these three statements have been interpreted with reference to the Trinity. The Father is seen in the words 'God created'. The Spirit is seen in the words referring to 'the Spirit of God'. The Son is seen in the words 'Then God said...' The last interpretation is justified in the light of John 1:1–4, where Jesus is called 'the Word' (linking him to 'God said') and the 'light of all people' (linking him to 'let there be light').

Christians therefore believe that God created the world and that this creative work involved the three persons of the Godhead together: the Father as source, the Son as instrument, the Spirit as energizer. Accordingly, the universe was created by God, but God understood in the uniquely Christian sense of Father, Son and Holy Spirit.

The universe was created over time

As you read Genesis 1 it becomes clear that creation is being portrayed as a divinely orchestrated *process*. The events of creation unfold over a period of six days. The big question for most people is this: 'Does a day in Genesis 1 signify a literal twenty-four-hour time frame? Or does it signify a much longer period of time, like an "age"?'

There are two common answers to this question.

There is first the answer of the person who takes the word 'day' literally. They argue that there is nothing in the context of the passage itself to suggest that a day is anything other than a day in the normal sense of the word. The days begin in the evening and end in the morning. This sounds like a day! Furthermore, people who defend the literal reading of 'day' argue that it is only the theory of evolution that encourages an interpretation of 'day' as an epoch or longer. If we didn't know about evolution we wouldn't think of 'day' metaphorically.

Those who believe in the literal reading argue that the world was created by God in six literal days. They usually argue for a 'young earth', as it's called. In other words, they believe that the

world was created about 6,000 years ago.

The second answer is that 'day' should be interpreted metaphorically, not literally. Christians who follow this line of argument believe that 'day' refers to a period of time thousands, maybe millions, of years long. They see God's creation as something progressive – as something orchestrated by God over a long period of time, not in six literal days. They argue that even some of the early church fathers saw this (well before evolutionary theory was proposed). They show that the Hebrew word for 'day' (*yom*) is used

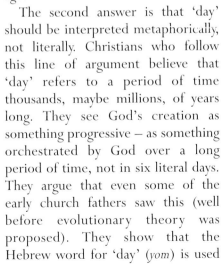

Three Christian views of creation	
Young earth creationism	The Genesis account is to be taken literally; the earth was created in six days and is 6,000 years old; the fossil evidence is misleading.
Progressive creationism	The earth is millions of years old and has developed progressively, not by chance evolution, but by special acts of God.
Theistic evolution	Life has come about by evolutionary processes for which God is responsible; the earth is constantly evolving under God's direction.

metaphorically elsewhere in the Old Testament; for example, the writer of Genesis switches from the word 'day' to the word 'generation' in Genesis 2:4, indicating that a longer period of time is implied in the word 'day' in Genesis 1. They point to verses such as Psalm 90:4 and 2 Peter 3:8, where the writers say that for God 'a thousand years are as yesterday', and 'a day is like a thousand years to the Lord'.

Those who believe in the metaphorical reading of the word 'day' argue that the universe was created over thousands or even millions of years. Far from believing in a 'young earth', those who believe in a progressive creation believe in an 'old earth' that is about four billion years old.

Whether you choose to believe in the literal, young earth creation, or the metaphorical, old earth creation, the fact is, the universe was created over time.

The universe was created in sequence

The next thing we may note about the creation account in Genesis 1 is that God creates things in a sequence: first light, then the firmament (separating sea and sky), then earth and its vegetation, then lights (sun, moon and stars), then fish of the sea and birds of the air, then beasts of the earth, and finally mankind.

It is again interesting to note how science and Scripture conform to one another here. For example, the writer of Genesis 1 says in verse 11 that God calls the land to burst forth with every sort of grass and seed-bearing plant. The word translated 'green grass' is *deshe* in Hebrew, referring to green matter. Today's scientists would call these 'chloroplasts', like algae. After 'every sort of green grass' comes 'seed-bearing plants'. These refer to what scientists call the 'cryptograms' (non-flowering ferns) and 'phanerograms' (flowering plants and trees). All these resulted in oxygen being put into the air.

'I find it as difficult to understand a scientist who does not acknowledge the presence of a superior rationality behind the existence of the universe as it is to comprehend a theologian who would deny the advances of science.'

Wernher Von Braun

The point is a simple one. God's Word says that the green grass and the seed-bearing plants appear *before* the creation of human beings. This is exactly what had to happen. The creation of the chloroplasts and cryptograms/phanerograms produced oxygen. You can't have human beings in an atmosphere where there is no oxygen! The sequence in Scripture conforms to the sequence discovered by many scientists.

Those who are not believers need to explain how an author writing 3,500 years before these scientific discoveries could ever have known about this sequence unless by God's 'special revelation'. Astrophysicists have recently proposed the following sequence: the creation of the physical universe (including space, time, matter, energy and stars), followed by the transformation of the earth's atmosphere, followed by the formation of a stable water cycle, followed by the formation of continents and oceans, followed by the production of plants, followed by the appearance of a transparent atmosphere (sun, moon and stars becoming visible), followed by the production of small sea animals, then sea mammals, then birds, then land animals, then mankind.

This sounds very similar to the sequence in Genesis 1!

The universe was created for humanity

The climactic act of God in the sequence described in Genesis 1 is the creation of human beings. In verses 26–27 we read:

> Then God said, 'Let us make people in our image, to be like ourselves. They will be masters over all life – the fish in the sea, the birds in the sky, and all the livestock, wild animals, and small animals.'
>> So God created people in his own image;
>> God patterned them after himself;
>> male and female he created them.

In Genesis 2:7 we read:

> And the Lord God formed a man's body from the dust of the ground and breathed into it the breath of life. And the man became a living person.

What becomes abundantly clear from this account is that God creates Adam and Eve at a particular moment in time. They did not emerge slowly out of a long process of evolution. Adam and Eve were created. They were not a highly evolved form of animal. They were created beings made in the image of God (see page 30), capable of relating to God in an immediacy of relationship – unlike animals.

Furthermore, everything that God did prior to this moment was for this moment. In other words, God created the universe and then the earth in order that Adam and Eve – the climax of his creative work – could live there. Genesis 1 shows God creating the heavens and the earth, the plants and the trees, the marine life and the animals, and then finally human beings. The significance of this sequence is this: the universe was created for human beings. The cosmos and the earth were carefully fashioned so that we could live in them.

Here again we can enlist the help of the sciences to support this. Astrophysicists argue that the universe may have started about 16 billion years ago and that the earth was formed about $4\frac{1}{2}$ billion years ago. Human beings appeared between 8,000 and 24,000 years ago. What scientists now believe is that the heavens and the earth were prepared as an environment for human beings to live in. Everything in the universe has been set up over millions of years to form the perfect habitat for human beings to live in.

Many scientists talk today about 'the anthropic principle', from the Greek word *anthropos* meaning 'man'. Cosmologists talk about the way the universe has been 'fine tuned'. Right from the singularity onwards, the particles and the quarks had human beings as their ultimate object and purpose. Every atom in our bodies was formed out of the dust from stars that exploded before the arrival of the sun and the earth. Human beings were part of God's plan from the beginning!

This means that the universe was created for you and me and that it is 'good' (a word used seven times in Genesis 1). So, for example, the strength of gravity in the universe is exactly what it needs to be for a planet the size of the earth to support human beings. Everything has been designed to suit human beings exactly. As God says in Isaiah 45:12, 'I am the one who made the earth and created people to live on it.'

God created a small home in a massive

> '**I refuse to believe the notion that man is flotsam and jetsam in the river of life, unable to respond to the eternal forever that confronts him.**'
>
> Dr Martin Luther King

Environmental stewardship

In the beginning, God called humanity to care for the earth (not to exploit it) and to name the animals. A number of Old Testament laws refer to the right stewardship of the land and to the need to give the land regular rest, referred to in the Bible as 'Sabbath rest' (Exodus 23:10–11). God also tells the Israelites not to pollute the land but to protect it (Numbers 35:33–34). These laws were designed to help human beings to serve their environment in a way that honoured God. Many Christians today believe that Jesus came to save the whole of creation, not just human beings, and that God plans to restore the cosmos to its original harmony (Hosea 2:18). They also argue that we are called to care for the earth and to respect and value other creatures with integrity. The Bible warns that lack of care for the environment evokes God's anger (Ezekiel 34:17–18). Caring for the earth is part of the Christian's stewardship.

universe just for us. As Arno Penzias, Nobel prize winner in Physics, has said:

> Astronomy leads us to a unique event, a universe which was created out of nothing, one with the very delicate balance needed to provide exactly the conditions required to permit life, and one which has an underlying (one might say 'supernatural') plan.

The universe is distinct (from the Creator)

There are two views about God and the world that present problems for many Christians. First of all there is deism, which argues that God is distinct from the world and no longer involved in it. In this view the world is like a watch and God is the watchmaker. God has made the watch but has now left it to run until it runs down!

Then there is pantheism, which says that God is not distinct from the world, and that the world and God are one. Here the world is regarded in relation to God as the body is in relation to the soul. The earth is God's body.

These two ideas are also known as dualism (in other words, that God and the world are a duality, separate and distinct) and monism, from the Greek word *monos* meaning one (the view that God and the world are one and the same).

Most Christians believe that both of these are inconsistent with the Bible. They believe that God created the world and that he is both transcendent and immanent. In other words, God transcends the world. He is above and beyond this universe, much greater than the sum total of all that he has made. At the same time, God is immanent; he is involved and active within creation, yet without being the same as creation. As we read in Jeremiah 23:23, ' "Am I only a God nearby," declares the Lord, "and not a God far away?" '

What Genesis 1 reveals is that God is both beyond and within the world that he has made. He creates the world but then in verse 31 he is said to look over all that he has made. This means that we can call God distinct from creation. At the same time, distinct does not mean 'uninvolved'. He has not left the watch to run down. He is still intimately involved with the running of the watch without the watchmaker and the watch becoming one and the same thing.

The universe God created is elegant

The climax of the creation account is the glorious revelation in Genesis 1:31, 'And he saw that it was excellent in every way.' Throughout Genesis 1 the writer tells us that what God made was good. Six times in fact! Finally, on the seventh occasion, we read that the Lord saw what he had made as 'very good'.

What is being celebrated here is God's elegant universe. God created something beautiful for human beings to inhabit – something so beautiful that he paused, looked at it and said, 'That's truly excellent.'

Perhaps that is why, in the final analysis, the writer of Genesis 1 gives us an account that is far closer to poetry than to science. It is in fact a beautifully designed piece of writing in itself. Note the structure of Genesis 1:1 to Genesis 2:4.

**Dear God,
In school we read that Thomas Edison made light, but in Sunday School they said you did it first. Did he steal your idea?
Sincerely,**
Donna, aged 8

What an elegance of description! The days of forming lead to the days of filling! What is formed on days 1, 2 and 3 becomes the environment for the creatures described in days 4, 5 and 6. The design of the whole chapter reflects the glorious harmony and order of the universe.

Forming	Filling
Day 1: separation of light/darkness	Day 4: sun, moon and stars
Day 2: separation of sea/sky	Day 5: marine life and birds
Day 3: separation of sea/dry land	Day 6: animals and humans
Day 7: God resting from his work	

All of this points to God creating the universe with elegance and with intelligent design. This is almost too hard for us to take in. As Albert Einstein once said:

> The human mind is not capable of grasping the universe. We are like a little child entering a huge library. The walls are covered to the ceilings with books in many different tongues. The child knows that someone must have written these books. It does not know who or how. It does not understand the languages in which they are written. But the child notes a definite plan in the arrangements of the books... a mysterious order which it does not comprehend but only dimly suspects.

Adam naming the animals, of North Midlands origin, twelfth century (vellum).

The role of faith

These wonderful truths about creation are not accessed by reason but by faith. As the writer to the Hebrews puts it:

> *By faith we understand that the entire universe was formed at God's command, that what we now see did not come from anything that can be seen.*
>
> Hebrews 11:3

What Christians believe about creation is not arrived at by reason but by faith. It comes from believing in God's Word through the illumination of God's Spirit. Some Christians believe that Genesis 1–3 is myth rather than fact (see the table above).

The 'Genesis 1 = myth' argument

1. The creation account in Genesis 1 cannot be historical because no human being could have been an eyewitness.

2. The creation account in Genesis 1 contradicts science when it says that everything was created in six literal days.

3. The creation account in Genesis 1 wrongly tells us that there was light before the sun and moon were created.

4. The creation account in Genesis 1 contradicts the account in Genesis 2 by having plants and animals created before humans (whereas in Genesis 2 humans seem to be created before plants and animals).

5. The creation account in Genesis 1 is too similar to ancient creation myths from other cultures to be regarded as historical.

Others believe (as I do) that there is nothing in the text to indicate that it is supposed to be regarded as myth, and that a literal interpretation (acknowledging where words are used metaphorically) does the best justice to the narrative and shows a surprising conformity to science.

Indeed, I agree with leading astronomer Dr Hugh Ross, who claims that 'the Bible is the only religious text that teaches a cosmology in full agreement with the latest astrophysical discoveries'.

4 The Fall

Have you ever wondered what's so special about human beings, what marks us out as unique in creation?

Christians believe that the uniqueness of humanity consists in the fact that we were made in the image of God (Genesis 1:26–27; James 3:9). What does this mean?

Let's take the subject of rationality. Unlike animals or plants, we are born with a natural capacity for reasoning. Where does this come from? It comes from God, who is the source of all that is wise, reasonable and true.

Then let's take the subject of morality. Unlike animals or plants, we are born with an innate sense of right and wrong. Where does this come from? It comes from God, who has a perfect sense of right and wrong, of good and evil.

Think about spirituality. Unlike animals and plants, we are born with a spiritual side to our nature – a part of our being that is designed to relate to God. This is because 'God is spirit' (John 4:24). The spiritual side of our nature is designed for communion with our Maker.

And finally, consider community or family. Unlike animals and plants, human beings are able to communicate and commune with one another in love, in marriage and as family. Where does this come from? It comes from God, who is forever in his own being a family of three persons in one being.

We were created to reason wisely, to think and act rightly, to relate to God intimately and to love one another deeply.

In addition, we were called to 'be fruitful and multiply' (Genesis 1:28). We were given the mandate to reproduce other human beings with a strong ability to reason, a strong sense of right and wrong, a strong relationship with God, and a strong love for others.

And last, but not least, we were called to care for our environment – to look after and watch over the animal, plant

and marine world and to lead the whole of the natural order in bringing glory to God (Genesis 1:28).

This is what it means to be made in the image of God.

Sounds wonderful! So what went wrong?

Falling from a great height

Christians believe that we were created to enjoy great heights of communion with God, with others and with the natural order, but that we fell from that original state of harmony into disharmony. This catastrophic loss of original innocence is known as 'the fall'.

'The fall' refers to the gap that has been opened up between what God wants us to be and where we find ourselves today. It refers to the great chasm between the pristine perfection of life in the Garden of Eden and the tragic disintegration of the world thereafter.

Genesis chapters 2–3 tell the story of how this fall came about. These chapters show how human beings misused their freedom and chose to disobey God.

Adam and Eve
Expelled from
Paradise
*c.1430–32.
Detail from
the Annunciation
by Fra Angelico
(c.1387–1455).*

God told Adam and Eve not to touch the forbidden fruit in the Garden of Eden. As Genesis 2:15–17 says:

The Lord God placed the man in the Garden of Eden to tend and care for it. But the Lord God gave him this warning: 'You may freely eat any fruit in the garden except fruit from the tree of the knowledge of good and evil. If you eat of its fruit, you will surely die.'

However, Adam and Eve disobeyed God and lost everything they had enjoyed before. As the writer of Genesis 3:23 puts it:

So the Lord God banished Adam and his wife from the Garden of Eden, and he sent Adam out to cultivate the ground from which he had been made.

Adam and Eve made a wrong choice and they fell.

The nature of sin

Christians believe that this wrong choice was the first or original 'sin' of human beings. Now 'sin' is a word that we don't hear very much any more. But while sin may be out of fashion as a word it is far from out of fashion as a way of life. So what is sin?

Sin is essentially a wrong attitude of mind. It is the attitude that says, 'I know best, not God.' It is the decision to live life in rebellion against God's law. It is self-rule rather than God's rule.

John Bunyan, author of *Pilgrim's Progress*, defined sin in a way that highlights this tragic note of autonomy and rebellion. 'So what is sin?' he asked. 'Sin is the dare of God's justice, the rape of His mercy, the jeer of His patience, the slight of His power, and the contempt of His love.'

Some may feel this is a little overdramatic. Surely sin can't be that serious? But from God's perspective this is an understatement not an overstatement. Sin is far more than an action that breaks God's moral law, though it is that too. It is a perverse attitude of the heart that says, 'I'll live life my way, not God's way.'

This is sin, and what Adam and Eve did was to commit the original sin. As the nineteenth-century American theologian Charles Hodge said, 'Original sin is the only rational solution of the undeniable fact of the deep, universal and early manifested sinfulness of men in all ages, of every class, and in every part of the world.'

> **'Sin may be defined as the personal act of turning away from God and his will... It is a personal spurning of the Lord of love... it is a betrayal of love.'**
> Professor Rodman Williams

The origin of sin

Where does sin come from?

Sin did not originate with God. God is completely holy – perfect and without sin – and he calls human beings to be holy. God cannot sin and he cannot either be tempted to sin or cause someone else to sin (James 1:13).

Deuteronomy 32:4 says it all:

He is the Rock; his work is perfect.
Everything he does is just and fair.
He is a faithful God who does no wrong;
how just and upright he is!

But if sin didn't come from God, where did it come from?

The Bible tells us that sin began with Satan, one whose name means 'adversary'. Many Christians believe that Lucifer – a chief angel – chose to rebel against God and fell from heaven, taking many other angels – known as fallen angels – with him. Those who hold this view interpret Isaiah 14:12–14 as a reference to this act of rebellion.

The Fall of the
Rebel Angels,
1562 (oil on
panel), by Pieter
Brueghel the Elder
(c.1515–69).
Musées Royaux des
Beaux-Arts de
Belgique, Brussels.

'How you are fallen from heaven, O shining star, son of the morning! You have been thrown down to the earth, you who destroyed the nations of the world. For you said to yourself, "I will ascend to heaven and set my throne above God's stars. I will preside on the mountain of the gods far away in the north. I will climb to the highest heavens and be like the Most High."'

What is interesting about these verses is the way in which Lucifer (whose name means 'Light Bearer') keeps saying the words 'I will'. This indicates that angels, like human beings, are created beings with free will. Lucifer and those who followed him chose out of their own free will to set themselves up against God. They chose to sin – to rebel against God and to opt for self rule rather than divine rule. As a result, they fell from heaven. Lucifer, the Light Bearer, became Satan, the Adversary.

Some Christians also believe that Ezekiel 28:12–19 refers to this great fall of Lucifer.

What these passages show is that sin originated with Satan. Satan sinned first and Satan experienced a 'fall' – a fall from heaven. Having fallen, Satan chose to express his rebellion further by tempting the parents of the human race. So we read in the first verses of Genesis chapter 3 that a serpent appears in the Garden of Eden. Satan is referred to in Revelation 12:9 as 'that ancient serpent who leads the whole world astray'. Clearly the serpent represents Satan.

Sin therefore originates with the disobedience of Satan. And Satan is portrayed throughout the Bible as an adversary who is real and must be resisted. The Catholic American Bishop Fulton Sheen once said these words: 'Do not mock the Gospels and say there is no Satan. Evil is too real in the world to say that. Do not say the idea of Satan is dead and gone. Satan never gains so many cohorts as when, in his shrewdness, he spreads the rumor that he is long since dead.'

Sin originated with Satan, and the Bible regards him as real.

The choice of sin

Why did Eve and then Adam give in to the serpent's invitation? The answer has to do with the seductive power of temptation.

There is an old saying, 'Give Satan an inch and he'll become a ruler.' Eve and then Adam gave space in their hearts to Satan. They only did this for a few moments but it was long enough to affect the whole course of history.

Why did this happen? The answer has to do with 'free will'. God gave human beings free will. He gave us from the beginning the ability to choose to love and obey him.

There are two phrases that the great thinkers of the early church used to employ in this matter. The first phrase is 'able not to sin'. The second phrase is 'not able to sin'. The fathers of the church recognized that God created human beings in such a way that we were able not to sin – if that is what we chose to do. We were never created as people 'not able to sin'.

The early church theologian Origen defined free will as a

faculty of reason that enables us to distinguish between good and evil, and a faculty of the will to choose one or the other. More recently, free will has been understood as the power to choose according to one's strongest motive, nature and character.

This is how God created the first human beings and this is how God created us. We are not robots programmed to please our Creator, like the women in the movie *The Stepford Wives*. We are human beings created with the capacity to reason and to choose. Adam and Eve were created with free will. Tragically, they chose poorly.

This raises the question, 'Did God know in advance that this was going to happen?' The answer is yes. God foresaw this wrong choice. He did not however cause it. Put another way, God allowed Adam and Eve to sin; he did not decree that they should do so. With regard to sin, God did not invent it and he did not prevent it. He regarded free will as such a precious gift and such a fundamental human right that he did not silence the serpent or control Adam and Eve. Love is always a choice. God allowed our first parents to choose, and they did not choose well.

The effects of sin

But surely all this is a fairy tale? It clearly isn't an eyewitness account of history since there were no other people to witness it! Surely Genesis 1–3 is the stuff of myth not fact. It's not meant to be taken literally.

There is a lot of debate about this issue. But many Christians hold the view that one of the golden rules of interpretation is this: the best interpreter of Scripture is Scripture. In other words, if you and I want to understand whether a passage is meant to be taken literally or metaphorically, then a good way to decide on that is to see how that passage is treated elsewhere in the Bible.

When it comes to the effects of the fall in subsequent history, a critical passage is Romans 5:12, which suggests that

The fall as myth not history

Some Christians do not regard the account of 'the fall' in Genesis 3 as an historical account but as a mythical story that the Israelites told in order to explain their sense of a broken relationship with God. This view regards 'myth' as something that may be true without necessarily being factual. Those who opt for this interpretation argue that it does not conflict with the evolutionary description of human origins and at the same time upholds the biblical view of humanity's need for reconciliation with God.

the apostle Paul regarded the fall as an historical fact. In this verse he writes:

When Adam sinned, sin entered the entire human race. Adam's sin brought death, so death spread to everyone, for everyone sinned.

It seems from this that Paul regarded Adam and Eve as real human beings who made a choice to sin. That first act of sin may have felt like a small step for the first human beings but it was a giant leap into darkness for subsequent mankind. As Charles I's chaplain Jeremy Taylor once wrote, 'No sin is small. It is against an infinite God, and may have consequences immeasurable.' He went on to add, using a very vivid image, 'No grain of sand is small in the mechanism of a watch.'

The consequences of Adam and Eve's sin were immense. As a result of their wrong choice, sin entered the human race. What this means is that every human being has been born separated from God and with the predisposition to self-rule. We are self-centred rather than God-centred from the beginning. We submit to self-rule and reject God, and run

'A little sin is like being a little pregnant. It will eventually show itself.'

Rick Warren

roughshod over the needs and rights of others. As Paul so powerfully puts it:

> *I know I am rotten through and through so far as my old sinful nature is concerned. No matter which way I turn, I can't make myself do right. I want to, but I can't. When I want to do good, I don't. And when I try not to do wrong, I do it anyway. But if I am doing what I don't want to do, I am not really the one doing it; the sin within me is doing it.*
> Romans 7:18–20

The inheritance of sin

But in what way does Adam and Eve's sin affect us today?

There are two main views about this. The traditional view, associated with Augustine of Hippo, is that the fall was an historical event, focused in a single act of disobedience, making all human beings guilty before God, and corrupting human nature. In this view, sin is both 'inherited' and 'imputed'. We inherit Adam's sin; all human beings are born into the world with a fallen nature. In addition, our solidarity with our first parents means that their guilt is debited to us too. Adam was our 'representative head'. What he incurred, we incur.

In stark contrast, a fourth-century British monk called Pelagius argued that Adam's sin only affected Adam. Therefore, we are not born with sin. We are born innocent and it is accordingly possible for a person to remain good and not need salvation. If we do sin, we choose to do so and in the process we follow Adam's example. In that case, Adam's sin is not ours. We are responsible only for the sins we ourselves choose to commit.

Going back to Romans 5:12, the traditional, Augustinian view is that sin entered the human race through Adam. This means that Adam's sin was not just an example of sin, without subsequent

> **The Eastern Orthodox view of original sin**
>
> The Eastern Orthodox Church has traditionally rejected the idea that the guilt of original sin is passed down through every generation. It bases its teaching on a passage in Ezekiel, which says a son is not guilty of the sins of his father. Ezekiel 18:20 reads, 'The son will not share the guilt of the father, nor will the father share the guilt of the son.'

effect on us. It means that Adam was the federal head of the human race and what he did affected the body of humanity.

Nature red in tooth and claw

The effects of the fall on human beings were catastrophic. As the sixteenth-century Puritan Joseph Alleine once lamented, 'O miserable man, what a deformed monster sin has made you. God made you little lower than the angels; sin has made you little better than the devils.'

The devastating results of human sin are seen first in the relationship between human beings. From Genesis 4 onwards there is what the Old Testament theologian Gerard Von Rad described as an 'avalanche' of sin. In other words, reading the final form of the text (Genesis 1–11) you are struck by the progressive and cumulative effect of original sin: Adam and Eve fall out with each other; Cain murders Abel; wickedness increases everywhere until the flood; and finally the Tower of Babel is built. One act of disobedience in the Garden of Eden affects all subsequent generations.

But the fall not only affects man's relationship to his fellow man; it also affects man's relationship to his environment. How does this happen?

This is a fascinating question and there are essentially two main answers to it. The first answer says that up until the fall of Adam and Eve, the whole of the universe was in perfect harmony. There were no earthquakes, no floods, no storms. There was no sickness, no suffering, no death. Everything was perfect. There were no signs of disorder, of nature being unruly, of a world 'red in tooth and claw'. However, after man's first disobedience, he fell and in the process he dragged the whole of creation with him. At that moment, suffering and death entered the cosmos for the first time.

The second answer is that the cosmos was already in a state of disharmony before the fall. When the devil and his followers fell from heaven, the effects were felt on earth too. So interconnected were the different parts of the cosmos that the rupture in heaven wrought destruction on the earth. What this means is that creation had already started to go wrong even before Adam and Eve's disobedience. The fall of the angels had caused disharmony in nature before the fall of humanity.

What is the evidence for this second view? There are a number of clues that the universe may have started to go awry even before the fall of humanity. Two are worth mentioning here.

There is first of all the serpent. What is a speaking, seducing snake doing in a supposedly perfect environment?

Secondly there is God's command that Adam should 'subdue' the earth (Genesis 1:28). Doesn't that imply there is something unruly that needs bringing to order?

Questions like these lead some to believe that creation was already imperfect even before the temptation of Eve and Adam. Something has already gone wrong if a serpent is acting so rebelliously and the earth requires subduing.

At 3,295 metres, Mount Etna is Europe's highest and most active volcano. July 25, 2001

So there are two answers. The first is the traditional perspective. The second is a more recent one. The attraction of the first is that it squares with what Christians have historically

believed and it also encourages us to take responsibility for the environment. The attraction of the second is that it clearly shows that humanity isn't ultimately responsible for environmental chaos (since creation is imperfect prior to Adam's sin), that there never was a perfect age in nature which palaeontologists need to locate, and finally – to quote my wife – that women ultimately aren't to blame for everything in the universe going wrong!

A critical belief

The doctrine of the fall is central to a true understanding of the Christian faith as a whole and the gospel in particular. It affects absolutely everything, as the apostle Paul explains in Romans and as other writers make clear throughout the Bible in its entirety. In many ways, what a Christian believes about the fall will tell you what they believe about everything else. As the American minister

R. A. Torrey once said, 'Tell me your doctrine of the fall and I will tell you the state of your theology.'

Some Christians have sought to deny that the fall ever occurred and that there was no original sin. They argue that there is original blessing instead, and that this God-given goodness still remains in nature and in human beings.

Other Christians have argued that evolutionary theory makes a literal Adam and Eve scientifically impossible and that the story of the fall is a religious myth.

Still others prefer to treat the account of the fall as a metaphorical description of the human condition – as a story that describes the existential condition of all human beings. In this view, the fall is not so much history as our story. The key thing is not that it happened but that it happens.

In response, Christians who hold a traditional view of the fall have argued that there are historical elements to Genesis 1–3 and that these should not be arbitrarily discarded. The narrative treats Adam and Eve as actual people, as does Jesus (Matthew 19:4) and the apostle Paul (Romans 5:12). Paul also compares Jesus, the second Adam, with the first Adam (1 Corinthians 15:45), implying that both are historical human beings. Furthermore, the New Testament writers speak of our original fall from innocence as fact not myth.

Whether you take a literal or a metaphorical view of the fall, however, the mainstream Christian belief is as follows: in the beginning, human beings were made in the image of God. This likeness to God was seen in at least four things: our rationality, morality, spirituality and community or family. As a result of the fall, we no longer think rationally, we no longer choose good over evil, we no longer put God first and we no longer love others selflessly. We are still made in the image of God, but sin has greatly distorted our likeness to the wonderful character of God. We have lost our communion with God, we have become polluted by sin, we fight one another, we pollute our planet and we die. This is bad news.

> 'There is no situation so chaotic that God cannot, from that situation, create something that is surpassingly good. He did it at the Creation. He did it at the Cross. He is doing it today.'
>
> Handley Moule

But there is good news too. Even though the first Adam sinned and we all sinned too, there is a second Adam. His name is Jesus. And the second Adam came to the rescue. In the next chapter, we will look at what Christians believe about Jesus.

5 Jesus

American astronaut Hale Irwin, after he had returned to earth having stood on the moon, said these words: 'The most significant achievement of our age is not that man stood on the moon, but rather that God in Christ stood upon this earth.'

If this is true, then it highlights how different the Christian faith is from all other faiths. This is not in any way to undermine or despise what others believe. It is simply to say that Christianity is built on this great claim: that in Jesus Christ God himself stepped down from heaven and stood where we stand. If other religions present human beings trying to climb up a mountain to where God is, Christianity reveals how God has come down from that summit and, in Christ, lived where we live and felt what we feel.

Jesus is therefore a unique figure on the stage of human history. Christians believe that Jesus Christ was human and divine. He was and is both fully God and fully man, in one person. As this God-man, he bridged the massive gulf between us and God, blazing a trail back to heaven for all those who choose to follow him.

This then is at the heart of what Christians believe – that Jesus Christ was 'Immanuel', God with us. It's a remarkable claim, of course, and it cuts completely against the usual human pattern. History, after all, is full of examples of men who would become gods. But it tells only one story of God becoming man. This story is the story of Jesus of Nazareth, which Christians believe is history.

In this chapter we will look at the following three subjects: the human nature of Jesus, the divine nature of Jesus, and what is referred to as the 'theanthropic' nature of Jesus (that is, his divine–human nature).

The human nature of Jesus

Few people today doubt that Jesus of Nazareth was a human being who lived in our history. Occasionally someone tries to argue that Jesus of Nazareth is just a legendary figure, that he didn't really exist. But in truth there is more evidence for the life and death of Jesus than for any other great figure of his age. In fact, there is more evidence for Jesus Christ than for another JC – Julius Caesar. No one doubts that Julius Caesar lived and died. Yet a few still claim this about Jesus. I suspect this is because it costs you nothing to believe that Julius Caesar said and did the things we read about. But it costs you everything to believe that Jesus taught and acted as the Gospels report. It's strange that, when you think about it.

Adoration of the Shepherds by Bartolome Esteban Murillo.

Let's just pause and verify that Jesus was indeed a human

being. What is the evidence for the human nature of Jesus?

First of all, there is his human birth. In Matthew's Gospel (chapters 1 and 2) we learn all about how Jesus was born. The same is true of Luke's Gospel (chapters 1 and 2). Both Gospels begin with what are called 'infancy narratives', that is, stories about Jesus' infancy. Luke, who was meticulous about his historical research, wrote that Mary 'gave birth to her first child, a son. She wrapped him snugly in strips of cloth and laid him in a manger, because there was no room for them in the village inn' (Luke 2:7). Matthew says, 'Jesus was born in the town of Bethlehem in Judea, during the reign of King Herod' (Matthew 2:1). This is the great message of Christmas: that Jesus Christ was born nearly 2,000 years ago to be our Saviour.

Secondly, there is Jesus' development. Luke records that the twelve-year-old Jesus 'grew both in height and in wisdom, and he was loved by God and by all who knew him' (Luke 2:52). What Luke is recording here is that Jesus grew physically (in height), intellectually (in wisdom), spiritually (in relationship with God) and socially (in relationship with those who knew him). Jesus did not arrive on the earth fully grown, a thirty-year-old man, fully formed and mature at every level. No, he spent his childhood and youth developing in all the ways that we are meant to.

Thirdly, there is Jesus' human family. Jesus grew up as a Jewish child in a Jewish family. We see this at the beginning of Mark chapter 6 when Jesus returns as an adult to the place where he grew up – Nazareth. He comes back to his family home and goes to preach at the local synagogue where he worshipped as a boy. Many of those who hear him are said to be astonished: 'Where did he get all his wisdom and the power to perform such miracles? He's just the carpenter, the son of Mary and brother of James, Joseph, Judas, and Simon. And his sisters live right here among us' (Mark 6:2–3). Whatever else these verses reveal, they show that people knew Jesus had grown up in a family in his hometown of Nazareth.

> 'When Jesus is viewed as a Jew, within the context of first-century Judaism, an entirely different portrait emerges.'
>
> Brad Young

The Jewishness of Jesus

- Jesus was born to devout Jewish parents
- Jesus was circumcised on the eighth day after his birth
- Jesus was given a Hebrew name, one of the five most popular names for Jewish boys in his day
- Jesus observed Shabbat (the Sabbath) and attended the local synagogue
- Jesus observed the Jewish festivals
- Jesus went up to Jerusalem every year for Passover
- Jesus studied the Torah (the Jewish Scriptures)
- Jesus, at twelve years old, dialogued with the Jewish sages in Jerusalem
- Jesus was recognized as Jewish by Jews and non-Jews alike
- Jesus used parables and other familiar teaching methods of the Jewish sages
- Jesus was well versed in the Jewish Scriptures and able to refer to them in his teaching
- Jesus spoke in Aramaic
- Jesus' favourite theme was 'the kingdom of heaven'
- Jesus' model prayer (the Lord's Prayer) used themes from the Jewish Prayer Book of his day
- Jesus was referred to as 'Rabbi', a term of respect (and not a reference to an ordained office)
- Jesus died as a Jew, with the Psalms on his lips.

Fourthly, there is the evidence of Jesus' human emotions. It is simply not true to say (as some have) that Jesus is portrayed in the Gospels as an aloof deity, walking around without any human feelings whatsoever. This is a major distortion of the true picture. Jesus is said to be amazed and surprised on one occasion (Matthew 8:10). He is described showing anger (John 11:35). He is portrayed as being troubled and anxious, not least about his imminent crucifixion (John 12:27; 13:21). He says in the Garden of Gethsemane that his soul is crushed with grief (Matthew 26:38). This is not the behaviour of a god who knows nothing of the commonest human emotions.

Fifthly, there is the evidence of Jesus' human experiences. Jesus had human needs, just as we do. In John 4:6 he is said to be tired. In Matthew 4:2 he is said to be hungry. In John 19:28 he is said to be thirsty. Again, this is a thoroughly human Jesus!

Sixthly, there is the evidence of Jesus' human temptations. The Bible says of Jesus that he was tempted in every way just as we are, except that he didn't give in to temptation (Hebrews 4:15). He was presented with the opportunity to sin but he said no every time. In fact, Jesus lived a completely sin-free life from his birth to his death. For the first time in history, a human being managed to resist temptation during the entire course of his life. He could have sinned, but he chose not to. What an amazing achievement!

Finally, there is the evidence of Jesus' human death. One thing is for sure: human beings die. We all have an appointment with death. Sooner or later it is going to happen to every single one of us. And it happened to Jesus too, which is a big comfort. As it says in Hebrews 2:14–15:

> Because God's children are human beings — made of flesh and blood — Jesus also became flesh and blood by being born in human form. For only as a human being could he die, and only by dying could he break the power of the devil, who had the power of death. Only in this way could he deliver those who have lived all their lives as slaves to the fear of dying.

So, there are at least seven pieces of evidence concerning Jesus' human nature: his birth, his development, his family, his emotions, his experiences, his temptations, and his death. Jesus was completely human in nature. As Rob Bell puts it, 'Before all the big language and the grand claims, the story of Jesus was about a Jewish man, living in a Jewish region among Jewish people, calling people back to the Jewish God.' No one doubted Jesus' humanity in his own day. We shouldn't today either.

The divine nature of Jesus

One of the most common challenges to Christianity being made in our times is that the divinity of Jesus was something invented hundreds of years after Jesus had lived and died. It is being argued more and more that 'divinity' was not something that Jesus claimed for himself, or demonstrated; rather it was ascribed to him by later Christians, who turned a Jewish prophet into a Gentile god. This is one of the themes of the novel *The Da Vinci Code*.

In reality, the divinity of Jesus is presupposed in over 500 verses of the New Testament and explicitly claimed at a number of points. In other words, Jesus is spoken of as divine within a few years of his death – not three centuries afterwards!

Let me again point to just a sample of the biblical evidence that Jesus was much more than just a human being – that he had what we might call a divine nature as well.

First of all there is the evidence of Jesus' divine pre-existence – the idea that Jesus existed prior to his birth. This is particularly striking in the episode recorded in John 8:31–59. Here Jesus engages in a very heated exchange with some fellow Jews. John records that the argument reaches a terrifying finale when Jesus makes the provocative claim, 'Before Abraham existed, I am' (John 8:58). Now there are two things that are inflammatory here: Jesus' claim that he had been alive 1,500 years before this conversation – before Abraham (the beloved patriarch of the accusers here) was born; and Jesus' use of the phrase 'I am' – a name for God in the Old Testament. This is all too much for Jesus' listeners, who try to stone him.

> 'In order that the body of Christ might be shown to be a real body, he was born of a woman. In order that his Godhead might be made clear, he was born of a Virgin.'
> Thomas Aquinas (1225–74)

There is secondly the evidence of Jesus' divine conception. In Luke 1:26–38 we read how the angel Gabriel visits Mary – a young Jewish girl who has never had sexual relations with her fiancé Joseph or any other man. The angel tells her that she is going to have a baby boy called Jesus. Mary is startled and asks how this is possible because she is a virgin. The angel replies that this baby is going

Annunciation
(c.1410–40) by
Robert Campin.

There's something about Mary

All Christians agree that Mary was the mother of Jesus and was especially chosen for the task. In the early church, two factors caused her to be elevated in people's understanding. First, that Mary had been a virgin when she conceived led some to say that she was forever pure (a view known as 'the perpetual virginity of Mary'). This idea was developed in the Middle Ages to become the doctrine of the 'immaculate conception' – the view that Mary was born without sin – and eventually became an official doctrine of the Catholic Church in 1854. Secondly, that Mary had carried God's Son in her womb led to her description as *Theotokos* ('God Bearer' or 'Mother of God'). This elevation of Mary led many Roman Catholics to pray to her as a mediator, and to argue that Mary did not die but was taken up into heaven. This is known as 'the doctrine of the bodily assumption of Mary' and became a dogma in 1950. After the Reformation Protestants questioned these beliefs, arguing that Christians should only pray to Jesus, as he is the true mediator. Today, all Christians regard Mary as an example of great devotion to God.

to be conceived through the work of the Holy Spirit and will be called 'the Son of God'. Mary obediently accepts her calling and later gives birth to Jesus as a result of divine rather than human intervention in the process of conception. Jesus is therefore conceived miraculously.

There is thirdly the evidence of Jesus' divine authority. In many places Jesus speaks as if he is God. In Matthew chapter 5 he tells his listeners that his words have greater authority than those of Moses. He says to his contemporaries, 'I and the Father are one' (John 10:30). He tells people that he has the authority to forgive sins (Mark 2:8–11), something only God is able to do. His words of command calm the sea and the wind (Mark 4:41) and when he speaks, the dead are raised (Mark 5:35–43). Jesus has divine authority.

Fourthly, there is the evidence of Jesus' divine glory. On one occasion Jesus is with three of his closest disciples on the top of a mountain (Mark 9:2–13). These three are woken up to witness the radiating light of God's glory seeping out of Jesus' human body. This incident, known as the transfiguration of Jesus, is an important confirmation of Jesus' divine nature. Peter, who witnessed this, later wrote this in his second letter:

> We were not making up clever stories when we told you about the power of our Lord Jesus Christ and his coming again. We have seen his majestic splendour with our own eyes. And he received honour and glory from God the Father when God's glorious, majestic voice called down from heaven, 'This is my beloved Son; I am fully pleased with him.' We ourselves heard the voice when we were there with him on the holy mountain.
> 2 Peter 1:16–18

This is not a description of someone who has a purely human nature. The author of John's Gospel says, 'We have seen his glory'. John was also a witness of the transfiguration.

Fifthly, there is the evidence of Jesus' divine judgment. In John 5:22 Jesus clearly ascribes divine prerogatives to himself when he says that 'the Father leaves all judgment to his Son'. This is an unmistakable claim to divinity. Jesus is saying that he has the authority to do what God alone can do – to judge those who belong to God and those who do not.

Sixthly, there is the evidence of Jesus' divine titles. We have already seen how Jesus used the simple phrase 'I am' to describe who he was. Sometimes he used this with a qualifying description, such as 'I am the light of the world' (John 8:12). At other times he used it on its own – for example, 'When you have lifted up the Son of Man, then you will know that I am' (John 8:28). Jesus therefore used divine titles of himself. Others also used them of Jesus. For example, Thomas – who was said to have doubted Jesus' resurrection – eventually saw the risen Lord and proclaimed, 'My Lord and my God' (John 20:28). Perhaps most important of all is Jesus' description of God as Father and of himself as 'the Son'. See for example Matthew 11:27:

> *My Father has given me authority over everything. No one really knows the Son except the Father, and no one really knows the Father except the Son and those to whom the Son chooses to reveal him.*

These titles point to the possibility of a self-awareness of his divine nature.

Finally, there is the evidence of Jesus' divine resurrection. Whatever else we may say about the mysterious and miraculous event of the resurrection, one thing is to be emphasized here: that for the first Christians, Jesus' resurrection confirmed that he was the Son of God – that he was divine as well as human. As the apostle Paul said, 'Jesus Christ our Lord was shown to be the Son of God when God powerfully raised him from the dead by means of the Holy Spirit' (Romans 1:4).

Putting all these characteristics together – Jesus' pre-existence, conception, authority, glory, judgment, titles and resurrection – we have to conclude that the New Testament is not bashful about Jesus' divinity. Within the New Testament era (AD 30–100) there are many voices claiming that Jesus is divine. Take the apostle Paul for example. Writing in the AD 50s he says:

> *According to some people, there are many so-called gods and many lords, both in heaven and on earth. But we know that there is only one God, the*

> *Father, who created everything, and we exist for him. And there is only one Lord, Jesus Christ, through whom God made everything and through whom we have been given life.*
>
> I Corinthians 8:5–6

These words were not written centuries after Jesus. They were written only two decades after his death! They were written by Paul, a zealous Jew who became a Christian. That in itself is remarkable because monotheism – the belief that there is one God not many gods – was a very precious belief among the Jews. For a Jewish Christian like Paul to say that there is one God, the Father, and *in addition*, one Lord, Jesus Christ, is nothing short of amazing! Paul here is saying that Jesus Christ is divine, *in addition* to the Father. Here a Jewish monotheist (Paul) is saying that Jesus is 'Lord' – a word reserved for God. Something massive must have happened to make Paul think this way. Most likely it was the fact that Paul met the risen Jesus himself, on the Damascus Road.

The theanthropic nature of Christ

At the very heart of Christianity therefore is an amazing story – a story about Jesus. This story is His story; it is the history of God becoming flesh. A few years ago Joan Osborne released a song entitled 'What if God was one of us?' According to Christians, this has actually happened. In Jesus, God became flesh and became one of us. This truth, also known as 'the incarnation', is foundational to the Christian faith. Christians believe that Jesus was both fully divine and fully human, and that he is this for ever.

How, then, did these divine and human natures coexist in one and the same person? How could Jesus have had a 'theanthropic' nature? The word 'theanthropic' comes from two Greek words, *theos* meaning 'God' and *anthropos* meaning 'man' (or 'human being'). One of the most mysterious things about Jesus is how these two natures existed in unity. This question alone has kept Christians very busy for 2,000 years!

In what follows I am going to review some answers given in the first five centuries to the question of the two natures of Jesus Christ. This is only a very simple summary of the views concerned. The Christian church rejected these six views as wrong:

1. The Ebionite answer

The Ebionites were a second-century group who proposed that Jesus was fully human but not fully divine. In other words, he had no divine nature at all, only a human nature. They regarded Jesus as a man whom 'the Spirit of Christ' inhabited at his baptism, only to depart at his crucifixion. He certainly was not the pre-existent Son of God.

2. The Docetic answer

The Docetists were a group who arose late in the first century (represented by Basilides, Valentinus and others) who argued that Jesus was divine but that his human nature was not genuine. He appeared human but was not really so. In this view Jesus was fully divine but not fully human.

3. The Arian answer

The Arians, who followed Bishop Arius of Alexandria (fourth century), argued that Jesus Christ was more than human but less than God. Jesus was in fact a created being, albeit the first and highest created being – like the angels. It was this Arian view that the Council of Nicaea met to refute in the year AD 325 (and they voted 316 votes to 2 to reject it).

4. The Appollinarian answer

Named after Appollinarius (Bishop of Laodicea in the fourth century), the Apollinarians denied that Jesus was completely human. They argued that God's divine reason (known as the 'Logos') took the place of Jesus' human mind. Jesus had a human soul and body but his human mind was replaced by the divine Logos.

5. *The Nestorian answer*

Represented by Nestorius (fifth-century Bishop of Constantinople), the Nestorians denied that the two natures of Jesus were united. Jesus was two separate persons – a divine person and a human person. The divine person completely controlled the human one.

6. *The Eutychian answer*

During the third and fourth centuries AD, the church held several councils aimed at creating statements of belief around which the church could unite. The Council of Nicaea, which produced the Nicene Creed, is illustrated in the painting below by Cesare Nebbia (1534–1614).

Eutyches (fifth century) denied that there was any distinction between Jesus' divine and human natures. He argued that the human nature was swallowed up by the divine nature to create one nature – a third nature, if you will.

By the time of the famous Council of Chalcedon in AD 451, these six views had been robustly refuted by the theologians of the church. To combat them, the Council of Chalcedon arrived at what is known as the Chalcedonian Definition. This says: 'We teach people to confess one and the same Son, our Lord Jesus Christ, perfect in Godhead and perfect in manhood; truly God and truly man of a rational soul and body.' This statement goes on to say that Jesus Christ is 'to be acknowledged in two natures,

inconfusedly, unchangeably, indivisibly, inseparably'. It adds that the two natures existed in 'one Person… not parted or divided into two persons, but one and the same Son'.

Ultimately all this is a mystery. As the apostle Paul wrote, 'Great indeed, we confess, is the mystery of our religion. He was manifested in the flesh' (1 Timothy 3:16). Jesus Christ, the pre-existent Son of God, became a human being in the incarnation. Remaining what he was (divine), he became what he was not (human). This was an extraordinary act of humility. As Paul wrote in Philippians 2:6–8:

> *Though he was God, he did not demand and cling to his rights as God. He made himself nothing; he took the humble position of a slave and appeared in human form. And in human form he obediently humbled himself even further by dying a criminal's death on a cross.*

There is a story of a farmer who couldn't bring himself to believe this about Jesus – that though he was divine he had lowered himself to become a human being. One winter evening a snowstorm broke out. A flock of geese landed in his farmyard, disoriented by the strong winds. The farmer wanted to help them. He opened the doors of his barn to try and usher them

to shelter. He tried everything to get them inside but they became even more frightened. Feeling totally frustrated he cried out, 'Why don't they follow me? Can't they see this is a place of safety? How am I going to save them? If only I could become like one of them and communicate with them.' As soon as he said those words he suddenly understood what Jesus had done. Jesus had become one of us to save us. The farmer fell on his knees in the snow and worshipped Jesus.

No one can completely explain how the divine and human natures of

Jesus Christ coexisted in one and the same person. We will only know how in heaven when we cease to know in part. In the meantime, Christians go on believing and confessing that God's Son humbled himself and became a human being, and that he had a fully divine nature and a fully human nature united in one person. As to how, most are content to rejoice in the paradoxes rather than try and explain them away.

Having said that, Christians do continue to debate exactly how Jesus Christ could be both fully God and fully man. Some have relegated the language of Jesus' divinity to myth. Others have rigorously defended the fundamental historicity of what the New Testament claims about Jesus' deity.

The discussions carry on and will continue to do so!

In addition, Christians have been exploring the idea of 'kenoticism', from the word 'kenosis' referring to Christ's emptying of himself (Philippians 2:6–8). Some have argued that this self-emptying refers to Jesus voluntarily foregoing divine attributes in his human life. These vary from all of the divine attributes to just some (such as omnipresence, for example). Others have argued that this self-emptying refers to Jesus voluntarily restraining his divine attributes as a human being.

In the end, many Christians take the view that the New Testament talks about these issues in the language of adoring worship rather than metaphysical explanation. This means that most Christians are prone to celebrate the mystery rather than try and conquer it. Martin Luther said it well: 'The mystery of the humanity of Christ – that he sank himself into our flesh – is beyond all human understanding.'

6 The Cross

If our greatest need had been information, God would have sent us an educator. If our greatest need had been money, God would have sent us an economist. If our greatest need had been technology, God would have sent us a scientist. If our greatest need had been pleasure, God would have sent us an entertainer. But our greatest need was forgiveness, so God sent us a Saviour.

These anonymous words sum up one of the most fundamental Christian beliefs – that Jesus Christ was born to be our Saviour. Even the name of Jesus is significant in this regard. The name means literally 'God saves'. When the angel visits Joseph, he says this about Joseph's fiancée Mary: 'And she will have a son, and you are to name him Jesus, for he will save his people from their sins' (Matthew 1:21).

The purpose of Jesus' coming is therefore tied up in the word 'salvation'. Christians believe that what Jesus did on the cross dealt decisively with the problem of sin and reversed the effects of the fall. Christians believe that Jesus saved humanity at the cross.

> **'The whole of history is incomprehensible without Jesus.'**
> Ernest Renan

The passion of the Christ

All four Gospels build up to the climax of Jesus' suffering, death, burial and resurrection. In every case, a great amount of narrative space is given to the last days of Jesus of Nazareth. The earliest Christians knew that Jesus' death had changed everything. Their lives had been irrevocably affected by the passion of the Christ.

The phrase 'the passion of the Christ' has recently forced its way into the foreground of people's minds all over the world. The main reason for this is Mel Gibson's box office hit with the same

title. This became the most successful religious movie in history and one of the biggest blockbusters ever. People all over the world flocked to the cinemas to see a very graphic depiction of the last agonizing hours of Jesus' life.

And there is no doubt that Jesus went through agony. He first of all went through physical agony. He was stripped naked and whipped within an inch of his life. This torture was conducted by brutal Roman soldiers using short-handled whips that had nails and bones at the end of each strip of leather. Jesus then had a crown of thorns thrust upon his head. He was made to carry the *patibulum* or heavy crossbeam to a rubbish dump outside Jerusalem. There he had nine-inch iron nails rammed through the major nerves in his wrists and his feet (carefully avoiding arteries, lest he should die too quickly). He hung on the cross and slowly died of asphyxiation. To make sure he was dead, a spear was thrust into his side, piercing his lungs and heart.

Jesus suffered great agony physically. He also suffered great agony emotionally. He had to endure humiliating victimization by those who arrested and interrogated him, not to mention those who witnessed his final hours on the cross. He had to go through the rejection of his disciples' desertion. Only the beloved disciple and a few female followers stayed with him to the end. On top of that he had to face the personal agony of seeing his own family members, especially his mother, weeping over his sufferings. Jesus' agony was not just physical. It was emotional too.

And finally it was also spiritual. On the cross, Jesus experienced the absolute agony of feeling abandoned by his Father. Just before his death, Jesus quotes the start of Psalm 22. He cries out, 'My God, my God, why have you abandoned me?' Clearly something traumatic occurred in the consciousness of Jesus of Nazareth in the final moments of his life on earth. For the first and the only time, the constant intimate communion that he had enjoyed with his Father was fractured. Jesus felt bereft and forsaken. The one whom he called 'Abba', 'Dear father', had seemingly left him.

Jesus' passion (the word means literally 'suffering') was immense. It affected him at every level – body, soul and spirit. Jesus' death was quite literally excruciating.

Theories about the cross

But what was it all for?

While all Christians agree on the centrality of the cross, not all Christians agree on the precise reasons why Jesus had to die. Even today Christians have diverging views on how the death of Jesus 2,000 years ago affects us today.

There have been quite a number of views about Jesus' death since the earliest days of the Christian church. The ones that follow were rejected as too speculative.

1. The ransom theory

Some (such as the church father Origen) have seen the death of Jesus as God bribing or tricking Satan. This was rejected because it made God sound deceitful and the devil too powerful.

2. The recapitulation theory

Some (for example, the church father Irenaeus) have seen the stages of Jesus' life and death as a recapitulation and reversal of Adam's life and death.

Christ of St John
of the Cross
*(1951), by
Salvador Dali.*

3. The example theory

Some (such as Pelagius) have argued that the death of Jesus provides an example of faith and obedience to inspire human beings to live a holy and sacrificial life.

4. The moral influence theory

Some (for example, Abelard) have thought of the death of Jesus as the ultimate demonstration of God's love, which causes the human heart to soften in repentance.

5. The reward theory

Some (such as Anselm) believed that the death of Jesus brought infinite glory and honour to God; this led God to give Jesus a reward which he did not need, which he in turn gave to us – forgiveness.

While these and other theories concerning Jesus' death all have some merit, they have also been criticized as being in some way deficient in their attempt to explain what happened on the cross. So this still leaves us with the question, 'Why did Jesus die?'

Pictures of salvation

At the time of the millennium there was an art exhibition at the National Gallery in London that showed paintings of the life and death of Jesus Christ. The exhibition was called 'Seeing Salvation'.

When the first Christians preached about the cross they often used images or word-pictures to describe why Jesus had died. In Galatians 3:1, Paul says to the Christians in the church in Galatia, 'You used to see the meaning of Jesus Christ's death as clearly as though I had shown you a signboard with a picture of Christ dying on the cross.' From this we can perhaps infer that it was Paul's practice to paint a verbal picture of what Jesus had done at the cross. He used vivid images to depict the event and the significance of the death of Jesus. Through these images, Paul helped his listeners in the challenging task of 'seeing salvation'.

The New Testament contains a number of what we may call 'images of salvation'. These are word-pictures that are used by the New Testament writers to try and explain why Jesus died. They are, if you will, visual aids. The following five are the most significant and represent a more mainstream understanding of the cross.

A picture from the law court

Here the central idea is that of 'justification'. To be justified means to be declared 'not guilty' and 'innocent' before God – it means to be acquitted by God, the judge of the living and the dead.

The Bible teaches that all have sinned and fallen short of God's glory (Romans 3:23). However, God sent his only Son Jesus to die in the place of sinners. He had no sin in his life; he was absolutely perfect from his birth to his death. On the cross, Jesus Christ the righteous died for the unrighteous. He took the punishment that sinners deserved. He became, in the words of the Swiss theologian Karl Barth, 'the Judge judged in our place'.

Traditionally, it has been argued that justification achieves two things: a) it removes the sinner's unrighteousness; b) it replaces it with Christ's righteousness (this is known as 'imputed righteousness'). This means that when a person chooses to follow Jesus, God no longer sees their unrighteousness when he looks at them. He sees the righteousness of his Son. God imputes the righteousness of Jesus to believers.

All this serves to show that everything needed for salvation was done at Calvary. Christianity is therefore not about a 'Big Do'; it's about a 'Big Done'. Thanks to God's amazing grace, the work of salvation is finished. Humans cannot earn their salvation; that salvation has already been accomplished by Jesus. The part of the believer is to *trust* in the finished work of the cross. As Paul says in Romans 3:22:

> We are made right in God's sight when we trust in Jesus Christ to take away our sins. And we all can be saved in this same way, no matter who we are or what we have done.

In the light of this, the death of Jesus has huge implications. As unrighteous sinners, we are all under a sentence of death. But Jesus Christ came into the world and took the punishment for the sin of the world. He paid the price himself and died in the sinner's place. As a result, those who deserve judgment find themselves no longer in the dock but free. All who believe in Jesus are no longer under condemnation but under grace.

Justification is accordingly a vital concept. John Calvin described it as 'the main hinge on which salvation turns'. Martin Luther described it as 'the chief article from which all other doctrines have flowed'. Indeed, he argued strongly that when belief in justification falls from view, everything else falls with it. 'Without it', Luther said, 'the church of God cannot exist for one hour.'

A picture from the marketplace

The singer Johnny Cash once wrote a song called 'Redemption'. In it were these lines:

> The blood gave life to the branches of the tree
> And the blood was the price that set the captives free.
> And the numbers that came through the fire and flood
> Clung to the tree and were redeemed by the blood.

Slaves in chains on the island of Zanzibar in the nineteenth century. Slavery was abolished on March 5, 1873. Within twenty-four hours the main slave market on Zanzibar was closed and the slave trade was officially put to an end.

If the central idea of the law court image is 'justification', the central idea of the marketplace image is 'redemption'. In this word-picture the death of Jesus is seen as the means by which people are bought out of slavery to sin by the blood of Christ.

In biblical times, slaves were bought and sold in the marketplace. This practice influenced the way the biblical authors understood salvation. So, in the Old Testament, the great escape of the Israelites from their slavery in Egypt is seen as an act of redemption (see Exodus 6:6–8). In the New Testament, the rescue of all people out of slavery to sin is also seen as an act of redemption. So redemption language is found throughout the New Testament.

If you look below, the words on the left-hand side of the page are Greek words found in the manuscripts of the New Testament, and they all contain the idea of 'ransom':

lutron	ransom price	Matthew 20:28
antilutron	ransom price	1 Timothy 2:6
lutro	to redeem/ransom	Luke 24:21
lutrosis	redemption	Luke 1:68
apolutrosis	redemption	Colossians 1:13–14
lutrotes	redeemer	Acts 7:35

Redemption is a beautiful idea. In this word-picture, Jesus is the redeemer, the cross is the place of redemption, the blood of Christ is the payment, and sin is the slavery from which people are liberated. Jesus came to do what we are powerless to do. He came to set us free from our slavery to sin. That is why in Mark 10:45 Jesus said, 'the Son of Man has come not to be served but to serve and give his life as a ransom for many'.

Put another way, redemption says, 'I owed a debt which I couldn't pay. Christ paid a debt that he didn't owe.'

A picture from the Temple

If the central idea of the marketplace is redemption, the central ideas of the Temple are 'sacrifice' and 'substitution'.

In the Old Testament, God instituted sacrifices that were

designed to 'atone for' or cover over human sin. So, for example, lambs were slaughtered in the Temple precincts at Passover. Such imperfect sacrifices foreshadowed the superior way of dealing with sin: namely the sacrificial death of Jesus. This is why in the New Testament Jesus is portrayed as the true Passover lamb who died in the place of sinful human beings (John 1:29; 1 Corinthians 5:7; Revelation 5:11–12). His sacrifice is 'once and for all', as it says in Hebrews 9:26.

A key idea here is not just sacrifice but substitution, and what has been called 'penal substitution'. Jesus became humanity's substitute on the cross; as Martin Luther put it:

'We have a strange illusion that time cancels sins, but mere time does nothing either to the fact or the guilt of sin. The guilt is washed out not by time but by repentance and the blood of Jesus Christ.'

C. S. Lewis

Modern-day Samaritans sacrifice on Mount Gerizim.

'Our most merciful Father… sent his only Son into the world and laid upon him… the sins of all men saying: Be thou Peter that denier; Paul that persecutor, blasphemer and cruel oppressor; David that adulterer; that sinner which did eat the apple in Paradise; that thief which hanged upon the cross.'

Jesus took the punishment that is rightfully ours. As we read in Isaiah 53:4–6 (a sixth-century BC prophecy of the cross):

Yet it was our weaknesses he carried; it was our sorrows that weighed him down. And we thought his troubles were a punishment from God for his own sins! But he was wounded and crushed for our sins. He was beaten that we might have peace. He was whipped, and we were healed! All of us have strayed away like sheep. We have left God's paths to follow our own. Yet the Lord laid on him the guilt and sins of us all.

Christ's death was a substitutionary sacrifice that satisfied the demands of God's justice upon sin, paying the penalty for sin, bringing forgiveness instead of punishment.

A picture from the family

Here the key image used by the Bible is that of adoption.

Paul's letters mention the idea of adoption. In Ephesians 1:5 Paul writes that 'God's unchanging plan has always been to adopt us into his own family by bringing us to himself through Jesus Christ. And this gave him great pleasure.'

Paul was thinking as a Roman citizen here. In Judaism there was no rite of adoption; in Roman society children were often adopted. The usual scenario involved a couple who wanted a child but couldn't have one. The husband would approach one of the slave families in his villa and would petition a slave father for one of his sons. Subsequently, this father would take his boy to a magistrate. Here he would sell his boy to the man who wanted a child. This would happen three times before gold and silver were exchanged and the magistrate declared the child adopted. The child would then be regarded as the actual heir of his new adoptive parents' estate. He would no longer be a slave but a son – and a son with a new father, a new family, a new future and a new fortune. For this child, in an age when the life of a slave was indeed precarious, such an adoption would be true liberation. It could not be rescinded either. It was for life.

Paul had this picture in mind when he spoke about spiritual adoption. In his thinking Jesus has done everything required for believers to be rescued from slavery into sonship. He has bought them at a great price, not with gold or silver but with his precious blood. Now they are under the authority of a new father – the perfect Father. They are co-heirs with Jesus. As Paul puts it in Galatians 4:4–7:

> But when the right time came, God sent his Son, born of a woman, subject to the law. God sent him to buy freedom for us who were slaves to the law, so that he could adopt us as his very own children. And because you Gentiles have become his children, God has sent the Spirit of his Son into your hearts, and now you can call God your dear Father. Now you are no longer a slave but God's own child. And since you are his child, everything he has belongs to you.

At the heart of this theme of adoption is the idea of reconciliation. As a result of what Jesus has done on the cross, human beings are reconciled to the Father and they are also reconciled to one another. Through the cross, dividing walls of hostility (such as the barrier between Jew and Gentile) come crashing down and people begin to relate as adopted brothers and sisters in God's new family.

A picture from the battlefield

Lastly, the Bible draws on scenes from the battlefield to illustrate the idea of victory.

In 1 Corinthians 15:57, Paul declares, 'How we thank God who gives us victory over sin and death through Jesus Christ our Lord!'

The big story of the entire Bible is the story of a war between good and evil. This war begins in the Garden of Eden when the serpent (Satan) seduces Eve and Adam. Sin enters the cosmos and death takes hold. During the entire Old Testament era God's people remain under the oppression of the devil. With the coming of Jesus, however, the tide begins to turn. As Jesus begins his ministry, he ushers in the kingdom or the rule of God. This divine reign is inaugurated through words and works – through the authoritative words that Jesus speaks and the powerful works that he performs. As Jesus ministers, the devil's kingdom is pushed back. Jesus starts to deal blow upon blow against sin, suffering, sickness, oppression and death – against the toxic effects of the kingdom of darkness.

Then we come to the cross. Just before Jesus died, he said in John 12:31–32: 'The time of judgment for the world has come, when the prince of this world will be cast out. And when I am lifted up on the cross, I will draw everyone to myself.' Here Jesus anticipates that his death on the cross will result in the devil – the prince of this world – being driven out. This indicates that Jesus' death will deal a crushing blow against the devil. Far from being a defeat, the crucifixion will be a triumph. Here sin will be conquered and through the resurrection, death will be defeated.

After Jesus has returned to heaven (an event known as 'the ascension'), the Holy Spirit is poured out on the church at Pentecost (see page 104). The first Christians, endued with power from on high, continue to speak the words and do the works of Jesus. In the process, the fight against the kingdom of darkness continues. Every time the cross is preached and the power of the Spirit is demonstrated, the works of the evil one are pushed back and the frontiers of God's kingdom extended. All this continues until the last day of history when Jesus Christ will come back and evil will finally and completely be eradicated in the universe.

'The cross cannot be defeated, for it is defeat.'

G. K. Chesterton

Seen against this backdrop, the death of Jesus plays a critical role in the war against darkness fought out in the unfolding history of our universe. At Calvary, Christ appears to be the victim when in reality he is the victor. He is, as the Swedish twentieth-century theologian Gustav Aulen wrote, *Christus Victor*,

Christ the Conqueror. Aulen is talking about a 'dramatic' theory of salvation here. According to this theory the cross is the decisive moment of conflict between light and darkness, with the light overcoming the darkness. As Aulen puts it:

Celebrating V-E Day in Paris, May 8, 1945. Cheering Parisians line the Avenue de L'Opera as they celebrate the official announcement that the war in Europe is over.

> The work of Christ is first and foremost a victory over the powers which hold mankind in bondage: sin, death, and the devil.

Today we live between the first and second coming of Christ. As the theologian Oscar Cullman once remarked, the first coming of Christ is like D-Day. It is a critical blow against the enemy but it is not the enemy's final demise. That comes with V-E Day, which in Cullman's analogy is the return of Jesus Christ on the last day – the day of final victory. In the meantime the battles continue and the casualties are heavy. However, thanks to the work of the cross, we know that God understands our suffering and that the outcome of the war is not in any doubt. Evil may have its say, but God will have the last word.

Holy Communion

From the earliest days of Christianity, Christians have commemorated Jesus' death by taking bread and wine together. This is known variously as the Lord's Supper, Holy Communion, the Eucharist or the Mass. There is some debate over what happens when the bread and wine are taken, but most Christians believe the following things:

1. Holy Communion was established by Jesus (Matthew 26:26–28).

2. Jesus told his followers to continue to celebrate Holy Communion (Matthew 26:29).

3. Holy Communion proclaims the sacrificial death of Jesus (1 Corinthians 11:26).

4. Holy Communion confers some kind of spiritual benefit on the one who partakes of it.

The forgiveness of sins

Many views have been proposed in an attempt to explain what happened at the cross. Some of these have not found a consensus among Christians. Others – such as justification, redemption, substitution, adoption and victory – have become more mainstream interpretations. Even with these views, however, the debate continues. For example, there is a great deal of discussion about the exact meaning of 'justification'. There is also a great deal of discussion about the substitutionary idea of salvation (the 'satisfaction' theory), particularly the 'penal' aspect which portrays the Son as the object of the Father's wrath.

While Christians still discuss the finer details of these 'images of salvation', this does not mean that Christians doubt that Christ's death secures our salvation. They passionately believe that Jesus' death brings about atonement or 'at-one-ment'. This 'at-one-ment' is first of all between God and man. Jesus, the one who is fully divine and fully human, bridges the gap between the human and the divine in his saving death. At the same time, his blood brings about 'at-one-ment' between fellow human beings. It makes reconciliation possible between peoples who hate and

Differing views of Holy Communion

Roman Catholics call this 'the Mass'. They believe that when an ordained priest consecrates (or blesses) the bread and wine they are transformed into Christ's body and blood. This idea is called 'transubstantiation'. Roman Catholics also believe that at each Mass Christ offers himself to his Father just as he did on the cross at Calvary. The bread is given to every Catholic. In the past the cup of wine was withheld from those who were not ordained priests, but many churches now offer bread and wine to all participants.

Protestants tend not to believe that the elements of bread and wine change into Christ's body and blood. They do believe that Christ is present in these elements but not that he offers himself again, rather that his sacrifice is being remembered. This act of commemoration confers God's grace upon the recipients; it is spiritual nourishment. The bread and the wine are given to every church member, ordained and non-ordained alike.

destroy each other. Having been forgiven, people have a greater capacity to forgive others.

Ultimately, the significance of the cross lies in the fact that God freely and lovingly took the initiative in order to forgive sinful human beings. 'The forgiveness of sins' is a belief that lies right at the heart of the Christian faith in general and the cross in particular. Christians believe that God has done something extraordinarily loving at Calvary: he has extended a gift we didn't deserve, the gift of forgiveness. This, in brief, is what Christians call God's amazing grace.

And the cross is the greatest demonstration of God's grace. U2 singer Bono underlines this when he says, 'The thing that keeps me on my knees is the difference between grace and karma.' Asked by an interviewer what he meant, Bono replied that 'karma is all about me paying for my sins whereas grace is all about Christ paying for my sins'. The evangelical theologian Michael Green says, 'The Hindu doctrine of karma says, "You sin, you pay." The cross of Christ shows God saying, "You sin, I pay." And that is utterly unique!' Bono's conclusion is this: 'I'm holding out for Grace. I'm holding out that Jesus took my sins onto the cross, because I know who I am, and I hope I don't have to depend on my own religiosity.'

Christians believe in the finished work of the cross and celebrate it in the act of Holy Communion. Though they may have different ways of describing what happened at Calvary and why, in the final analysis all mainstream Christians believe that Christ died for our sins. They believe that the price for our sins was paid in full when Love was nailed to the cross. They believe that now, and in the future, they will be freely forgiven, not on the basis of their good deeds, but on the basis of Christ's saving death.

Christ's death on the cross was therefore for everyone. However, this does not mean that everyone will one day be saved and go to heaven (a view known as 'universalism'). The Bible teaches that human beings need to recognize that they are sinners and come to the cross in godly sorrow, putting their trust in the fact that Jesus died in their place.

Salvation is available to everyone. At the same time, however, repentance and faith are required from us if we are to avail ourselves of the benefits of the cross.

7 The Resurrection

The American Christian Peter Larson wrote this: 'The life of Jesus is bracketed by two impossibilities: a virgin's womb and an empty tomb. Jesus entered our world through a door marked "No Entrance", and left through a door marked "No Exit".'

That is precisely what Christians believe!

We have already looked at Jesus' birth in Chapter 5. In this chapter we look at the resurrection. To do that, we need to start with Jesus' burial.

After Jesus had died on the cross, he was buried in a tomb belonging to a rich man called Joseph of Arimathea. John records this event in some detail in his Gospel, pointing out that Joseph was a secret disciple of Jesus and a man of influence (John 19:38–42). Matthew adds that the tomb donated by Joseph was subsequently sealed and then guarded by Roman soldiers (Matthew 27:62–66). There was no way Jesus' body could have left that tomb by normal means. If ever there was a place marked 'no exit', this was it.

Yet the Gospels all report that on the third day after Jesus' burial, the stone had been rolled away and Jesus' body had gone. Jesus had been miraculously raised from the dead and angels had rolled the stone away from the entrance.

Joseph may have given Jesus the tomb reserved for his own burial, but Jesus only used it for a few days!

I like the apocryphal conversation between Joseph of Arimathea and a friend after the resurrection of Jesus. The story goes something like this. Someone said to Joseph of Arimathea, 'That was such a beautiful, costly, hand-hewn tomb. Why did you give it to someone else to be interred in?'

'Oh,' said Joseph, 'he only needed it for the weekend.'

Jesus did what was humanly impossible. On the third day after his death, he left a place marked 'no exit'.

The fact of the resurrection

There are a number of things Christians believe about the resurrection of Jesus Christ. First and foremost is the fact that it actually happened. Christianity is a faith based on God's actions in history. It is a faith based on factual events. Among the most important of these events is the resurrection of Jesus Christ from the dead. Jesus' resurrection is supported by two historical traditions contained within all four Gospels.

> **'The resurrection is perhaps the sole controversial Christian topic about which I would not desire to write... questioning the resurrection undermines the very heart of Christian belief.'**
>
> Dan Brown, author of *The Da Vinci Code*

The first of these traditions concerns the resurrection appearances of Jesus. The apostle Paul, writing within about twenty-five years of Jesus' death, said these words:

> *I passed on to you what was most important and what had also been passed on to me. Christ died for our sins, just as the Scriptures said. He was buried, and he was raised from the dead on the third day, as the Scriptures said. He was seen by Peter and then by the Twelve. After that, he was seen by more than five hundred of his followers at one time, most of whom are still alive, though some have died. Then he was seen by James and later by all the apostles. Last of all, as though I had been born at the wrong time, I saw him.*
>
> I Corinthians 15:3–8

Here Paul lists a number of people whom Jesus appeared to after his death, including Peter, five hundred followers on the same occasion, James, all the apostles, and last of all Paul himself. Paul is in no doubt that these appearances occurred. Indeed, he uses very technical religious language to describe this tradition – language reserved for the most sacred facts of Jewish history (for example, 'passed on'). Paul is convinced that the risen Jesus appeared to these people.

So there are accounts describing Jesus' resurrection appearances in the Gospels. Indeed Luke, a most meticulous historian, wrote this at the beginning of the book of Acts (volume 2 of his two-part work):

> *During the forty days after his crucifixion, he appeared to the apostles from time to time, and he proved to them in many ways that he was actually alive.*
> Acts 1:3

In addition to the historical tradition concerning the resurrection appearances, the New Testament reports the events that are the basis of the historical tradition concerning the empty tomb. The four Gospel writers state that a number of eyewitnesses found the tomb empty. They also reveal that the tomb was empty because the occupant, Jesus, had been raised! As Luke very briefly records:

> *Very early on Sunday morning the women went to the tomb, taking the spices they had prepared. They found that the stone had been rolled away from the entrance. So they went in, but they didn't find the body of the Lord Jesus.*
> Luke 24:1–3

The empty tomb tradition is the second, very strong piece of evidence that Jesus Christ had been raised from the dead.

The proofs of Christ's resurrection

The first Christians believed Jesus had risen from the dead and that he had appeared in bodily form among them. In Acts 10:39–41, Peter declares the following:

> *We apostles are witnesses of all he did throughout Judea and in Jerusalem. They put him to death by hanging him on a cross, but God raised him to life on the third day. Then God allowed him to appear, not to the general public, but to us whom God had chosen in advance to be his witnesses. We were those who ate and drank with him after he rose from the dead.*

Clearly Peter was certain about the fact of the resurrection. He had seen the risen Lord with his own eyes. Is it possible for us to be sure as well?

Let us consider some of the proofs for believing Jesus rose from the dead. Here are ten among many.

First, all four Gospels affirm the fact that Jesus rose from the dead. There is no contradiction about the main events. Jesus' body was no longer in the tomb on the first Easter Sunday because he had been resurrected. While the details may differ, the core event is preserved and proclaimed in all four Gospels. Given that these four Gospels come from different times and places during the first century, this common attestation is significant.

Order of the events of the resurrection

- Mary Magdalene, Mary the mother of James, and Salome start for the tomb, Luke 23:55–24:1

- They find the stone rolled away, Luke 24:2–9

- Mary Magdalene goes to tell the disciples, John 20:1–2

- Mary, the mother of James, draws near and sees the angel, Matthew 28:1–2

- Meanwhile Peter and John arrive, look into the tomb and depart, John 20:3–10

- Mary Magdalene returns weeping, sees two angels, then Jesus, John 20:11–18

- The risen Christ bids her tell the disciples, John 20:17–18

- Mary (mother of James) meanwhile returns with the women, Luke 24:1–4

- They return and see the two angels, Luke 24:5; Mark 16:5

- They also hear the angel's message, Matthew 28:6–8

- On their way to find the disciples, they are met by the risen Christ, Matthew 28:9–10.

MERRIL UNGER

Secondly, all four accounts give an unembellished report. There is absolutely no attempt to describe the actual moment when Jesus rose from the dead. The drama of that instant is not depicted (unlike the fictional, apocryphal 'Gospel of Peter', which provides an elaborate and exaggerated account). The restraint of the New Testament Gospel writers is a mark of veracity. It has a ring of truth about it.

Thirdly, the first witnesses of the resurrection were women. All four Gospels underline this fact. This is truly remarkable. At least three of the Gospel writers were Jewish. There is no way they would have portrayed women as the first witnesses had they been making it up. The testimony of a woman in a Jewish court was practically worthless. The presence and the role of these women is a strong argument in favour of the factual nature of these accounts.

Fourthly, the number of eyewitnesses is a strong argument in favour of historicity. The American theologian Merril Unger has listed the names of those to whom the risen Jesus appeared in the days after his death:

- To Mary Magdalene (John 20:14–18; Mark 16:9)

- To the women returning from the tomb (Matthew 28:8–10)

- To Peter later in the day (Luke 24:34; 1 Corinthians 15:5)

- To the disciples going to Emmaus in the evening (Luke 24:13–31)

- To the apostles (except Thomas) (Luke 24:36–45; John 20:19–24)

- To the apostles a week later (Thomas present) (John 20:24–29)

- In Galilee to the seven by the Lake of Tiberias (John 21:1–23)

- In an undisclosed location to 500 believers (1 Corinthians 15:6) and to James (1 Corinthians 15:7)

- To the apostles in the environs of Jerusalem (Acts 1:3–12)

This is an extremely impressive list. Many of these people would still have been alive at the time when the New Testament documents were being published. They could have refuted these claims had they been made up. But we find nothing of the kind.

Fifthly, the first Christians boldly proclaimed the resurrection. In the same area that Jesus was crucified, Peter stood up and said these words: 'God has raised this Jesus to life, and we are all witnesses of the fact' (Acts 2:32). It is not easy to see how Peter could have done this (in Jerusalem, in the Temple area) had he not been sure that Jesus was risen from the dead.

Sixthly, their Jewish contemporaries did not produce any counter argument. They could have spoken out against Peter's claim in Jerusalem, or subsequently, arguing that Jesus was not raised. But no such counter-arguments have been found.

Seventhly, the first Christians did not venerate the tomb of Jesus. The bodies of famous religious leaders and teachers were placed in well-known tombs that became the place of pilgrimage and worship, especially on the anniversary of the deaths of these figures. It is significant that there was no veneration of Jesus' tomb in the decades immediately after his death. The only plausible reason is that the disciples really did believe that the tomb was empty.

Eighthly, the early church made Sunday the highlight of the week. Up until that time, the followers of Jesus – who were Jewish – would have regarded the Sabbath (Friday evening to Saturday evening) as 'the queen of days'. But after Jesus' death, Sunday morning became the 'king of days' – the crowning moment of the week. The most plausible reason for this shift of emphasis was the belief that Jesus had been raised from the dead early on the Sunday morning of the first Easter Day.

Ninthly, the resurrection of Jesus explains the radical transformation of the disciples. Some of these men had deserted Jesus at the time of his arrest, trials and crucifixion. Peter had denied Jesus three times. But then, after Pentecost, we see him boldly proclaiming that Jesus is the Messiah (or 'Anointed One') and Lord. James, Jesus' half brother, doubted that Jesus was the Messiah in the time of Jesus' ministry. After Jesus' death, we see him as a leader of the church – a leader who is martyred because of his faith in Jesus. How do we account for such extraordinary changes in belief? The best answer is that these disciples – and many others besides – saw the risen Jesus and from that moment on were convinced that Jesus was the Messiah.

Tenthly, the personal experience of billions of Christian attests to the fact that Jesus is risen from the dead. Simply put, there are nearly two billion people alive today (and this number is growing dramatically) who believe in their hearts that Jesus is risen from the dead and confess with their mouths that Jesus is Lord. There is a vast family of people across the globe that worships Jesus, believing that he is far more than a great teacher or a great prophet, that in fact he is the Lord of heaven and earth. How could this be unless he really was and is alive?

In the light of these and many other arguments, it takes greater faith to say that the resurrection was invented than it does to say that it actually occurred!

The nature of Christ's resurrection

What kind of body did Jesus have after his resurrection from the dead?

The first thing to say is that it was a physical body. Peter, in his speech in Acts 10 (see page 93), says that Jesus ate and drank with him (and the other disciples) after the resurrection. This confirms what Luke records in volume one of his two-volume history. In the Gospel of Luke he records the moment when the risen Jesus appears to his disciples:

> 'Look at my hands. Look at my feet. You can see that it's really me. Touch me and make sure that I am not a ghost, because ghosts don't have bodies, as you see that I do!'
> As he spoke, he showed them his hands and his feet.
> Luke 24:39–40

Clearly, Jesus' resurrection body is a physical body, still carrying the scars of the crucifixion. As if to underline the physicality of this body, Luke further reports:

> Still they stood there in disbelief, filled with joy and wonder. Then he asked them, 'Do you have anything here to eat?' They gave him a piece of broiled fish, and he ate it as they watched.
> Luke 24:41–43

Jesus' resurrection body was a physical body that could be seen and touched. It was a body that could consume food and drink. Jesus did not transition into a disembodied state after his death. He was raised in bodily form.

At the same time this body was also a spiritual body. The evidence for this is the mysterious way in which the risen Jesus could suddenly appear in the presence of his disciples (Luke

24:36), including in rooms where the doors were locked (John 20:19). This suggests that the risen Jesus had entered a new mode of existence. His body was a spiritual body. While there was a continuity between his life before and after the resurrection, there was also a strange otherness about his new, spiritual body.

This is further indicated by the fact that some of the disciples occasionally had difficulty recognizing the risen Jesus, even though they had been with him for up to three years beforehand. Most notable of all these examples is the one involving Mary Magdalene in John 20:12–18. Mary Magdalene is weeping at the empty tomb when John records the following:

Noli Me Tangere (Do not touch me) by Fra Angelico and Workshop, 1425–30.

> *She turned to leave and saw someone standing behind her. It was Jesus, but she didn't recognize him.*
>
> *'Dear woman, why are you crying?' Jesus asked her. 'Who are you looking for?' She thought he was the gardener. 'Sir,' she said, 'if you have taken him away, tell me where you have put him, and I will go and get him.'*

The conclusion Christians draw from incidents like this is not that the person in these episodes is someone different from Jesus. Rather, they conclude that Jesus' resurrection body was a spiritual body. It was so radiant with the glorious life of heaven that it was sometimes hard to recognize.

All this highlights the miraculous and supernatural nature of the resurrection of Jesus. Some people over the years have tried to provide alternative theories of the resurrection story. They have proposed that those who saw Jesus were in a swoon, or hallucinating. Others have tried to prove that the whole story was in fact a great conspiracy, or a myth invented by the first disciples. None of these theories has been as convincing as the more conventional, Christian belief stated here.

The problem with many of the sceptical views of the resurrection is that they come from people who operate with a naturalistic worldview. Naturalism – also known as materialism – is a way of thinking in which everything is explained by natural causes. Physical matter is the only reality. Naturalism therefore excludes the possibility of any supernatural cause or activity in the world.

Most sceptical views of the resurrection are the product of a prior commitment to naturalism. However, the Christian worldview is not a naturalistic worldview. While it embraces the physical and the material, it also makes room for the supernatural and the spiritual. Christians believe that the most cogent explanation of the resurrection of Christ is a supernatural one. They believe that Jesus Christ was raised from the dead by the glorious power of the Father (Romans 6:4). The resurrection of Christ cannot therefore be reduced to a purely naturalistic explanation.

The centrality of Christ's resurrection

Christians believe that the resurrection of Christ is an absolutely central and critical historical event and article of faith. As the apostle Paul says in 1 Corinthians 15:17, 'If Christ has not been raised, then your faith is useless, and you are still under condemnation for your sins.' In other words, if the resurrection of Christ is a myth, then the whole system of the Christian faith implodes. It is absolutely essential. Christ not only died (thereby defeating sin), he also rose from the dead (thereby conquering death). The resurrection of Jesus Christ changes everything.

'Without the resurrection, our faith is dead. The story's not complete without it.'

Mel Gibson

First of all it changes everything as far as Christ is concerned. The Bible teaches that in the act of resurrecting Jesus of Nazareth, God the Father vindicates and confirms

Jesus as his Son (Romans 1:4). Not only does the resurrection confirm the fact that Jesus really died; it also confirms the fact that Jesus was not a liar, or a lunatic, but Lord (to use C. S. Lewis's famous categories). To the first Christians, it was the resurrection that convinced them that Jesus Christ was and is divine. No other Messianic figure had ever been raised from death, nor were they expected to be. Jesus is utterly unique in this regard.

Secondly it changes everything as far as Christians are concerned. The same power that raised Jesus from death – the power of God's Holy Spirit – is now at work within the followers of Jesus. The Holy Spirit (whom we will look at in the next chapter) is the power of the age to come. Christians believe he is at work in their mortal bodies today, giving them a foretaste of what the kingdom of heaven will be like when Jesus Christ returns. He fills believers with hope concerning their eternal future, saying in effect, 'If Jesus was raised, so will you be who follow him.'

> '**Because of Easter, our coffins are nothing but canoes bearing us across the Jordan River to fairer worlds on High.**'
>
> Herman Melville, *Moby Dick*

It thirdly changes everything as far as God's creation is concerned. Through the bodily resurrection of Christ, the power of heaven has infiltrated the particles of this earth. In the momentous event of the resurrection, the life of the future age has arrived ahead of time and invaded our material world. Death has been defeated and the effects of the fall have started to be reversed. On the first Easter morning, a day of new creation therefore dawned for the cosmos. The resurrected body of Jesus is the sign of how the world will one day look. Just as Jesus' spiritual body was both continuous and discontinuous with his human body, so the new  creation will be both the same as and different from the old creation. One day Jesus will make all things new, even as he was made new.

It is hard not to conclude that the resurrection of Christ is central to Christianity. Right from the word 'go', the first Christians testify to the resurrection. All nine sermons in the book of Acts focus on the resurrection of Christ. It was the focus of the good news that they were called to preach.

Today it is just the same: the resurrection of Christ is central to what Christians believe. And, as the American philosopher William Craig Lane has said, 'Whatever they may think of the historical resurrection, even the most skeptical scholars admit that at least the belief that Jesus rose from the dead lay at the very heart of the earliest Christian faith. In fact, the earliest believers pinned nearly everything on it.'

8 The Holy Spirit

The Gospel of Luke ends with the risen Jesus appearing to his disciples. The final words of Luke chapter 24 tell us what happened to Jesus at the very end of his time on earth 2,000 years ago. In verses 50–53 Luke reports:

Then Jesus led them to Bethany, and lifting his hands to heaven, he blessed them. While he was blessing them, he left them and was taken up to heaven. They worshipped him and then returned to Jerusalem filled with great joy. And they spent all of their time in the Temple, praising God.

According to Luke, Jesus was 'taken up to heaven'. After forty days of appearing to the disciples, the risen Jesus was elevated into the sky while he was praying for them. At the start of his second volume, the book of Acts, Luke tells us that 'Jesus was taken up into a cloud while they [the disciples] were watching, and they could no longer see him' (Acts 1:9).

This event is known as the ascension. Christians believe that the risen Jesus is not still going about somewhere on the earth, but that he left and returned to his Father in heaven. This journey home was obviously something that transcended all human categories. The Son of God was taken up to his Father in heaven supernaturally by the Holy Spirit. This was an event of such reality and wonder that it resulted in a whole new understanding of who Jesus was for the disciples. This accounts for Luke's words, 'they worshipped him'. It also accounts for their 'great joy' after his departure (when we would have expected great sadness). And it explains Peter's bold and fearless declaration that 'Now Jesus sits on the throne of highest honour in heaven' (Acts 2:33).

Christians believe that Jesus died and that he rose again (the doctrine of the resurrection). Christians believe not only that Jesus rose again, but that he was also taken up into heaven (the doctrine of the ascension). And Christians believe not only that he was

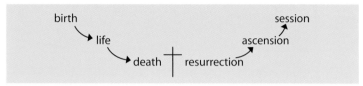

taken up into heaven, but also that he sat down at the right hand of the Father, showing that his work is now complete (the doctrine of the session of Christ). The charismatic theologian Professor Rodman Williams puts it well: 'Jesus went to an absolutely inaccessible sphere that no telescope however powerful can see and that no space vehicle regardless of its speed can ever reach.'

The diagram above depicts something of the journey of Jesus Christ from his incarnation (birth as a human being) to his ascension and session.

The ascension is a wonderful doctrine. As Professor Tom Torrance has said, 'In the incarnation we have the meeting of man and God in man's place, but in the ascension we have the meeting of man and God in God's place.'

The promise of the Holy Spirit

Just before his ascension, Jesus promised his disciples that they would receive the 'Holy Spirit'. He told them not to leave Jerusalem but to wait for the Holy Spirit to 'baptize' them (Acts 1:5). The word 'baptize' means to drench or soak. What Jesus was promising was a totally immersive experience of the empowering presence of God. This power would mobilize the disciples and send them out to be witnesses to Jesus locally, regionally, nationally and globally (Acts 1:8).

And that's precisely what occurred. Ten days after the ascension, on the day of the Jewish Feast of Pentecost, the Holy Spirit overwhelmed the disciples. Luke records the event vividly in Acts 2:2–4:

> *Suddenly, there was a sound from heaven like the roaring of a mighty windstorm, and it filled the house where they were meeting. Then, what*

looked like flames or tongues of fire appeared and settled on each of them. And everyone present was filled with the Holy Spirit and began speaking in other languages, as the Holy Spirit gave them this ability.

Pentecost, *from the Gospel and Epistle Lectionary (St Trond Lectionary)*.

Having ascended into the heavens, Jesus pours out the Holy Spirit from the right hand of the Father (Acts 2:33). The ascended Jesus is accordingly the Lord of the Spirit.

All this encourages the question: Who, or what, is 'the Holy Spirit'? In the next few pages we will look at five things the Bible claims about the Holy Spirit.

The Holy Spirit is personal

A Sunday school class was studying the Apostles' Creed (see the introduction). Each person in the class was given a section of the creed to learn by heart. Every Sunday the children were to take it in turns to recite their part by heart. The next Sunday the class began. A child stood up and said, 'I believe in God the Father Almighty, maker of heaven and earth.' Another child stood up and said, 'I believe in Jesus Christ, his only Son our Lord.' Then there was a long pause. Finally a girl stood up and said, 'I'm sorry, miss, but the boy who believes in the Holy Spirit isn't here today.'

> 'Long before the Holy Spirit became an article of the Creed, he was a living reality in the experience of the early church.'
>
> Eduard Schweizer

Christians believe that the Holy Spirit is personal – that he is the third person of the Trinity.

This is not an easy concept to grasp. People hearing the phrase 'the Holy Spirit' are apt to think that an impersonal power is

The Pentecostal Movement

The worldwide Christian movement known as Pentecostalism takes its name from the day of Pentecost, when the Holy Spirit fell upon Jesus' disciples as they were gathered in Jerusalem (Acts 2). Pentecostals believe that the Holy Spirit comes upon Christians today. This event (subsequent to conversion) is known as 'baptism in the Holy Spirit' and is often attended by spiritual gifts such as speaking in tongues. The gifts of the Spirit are described in 1 Corinthians 12:1–11 – a list that includes the gifts of miracles and prophecy. Pentecostals believe that all of these spiritual gifts are available to Christians today. Ever since the outpouring of the Holy Spirit at Azusa Street Los Angeles in 1906 (the birthplace of Pentecostalism), Pentecostal Christianity has continued to place a marked emphasis upon the supernatural dimension of Christianity. Believers who feel an allegiance to Pentecostalism number in excess of 500 million today.

being referred to, something akin to the mystical 'force' in the *Star Wars* movies. It is easy to see how 'the Father' is personal. It is easy to see how 'the Son' is personal. But the words 'the Holy Spirit' sound far more impersonal. How can it be that 'the Holy Spirit' is a person?

There are a number of reasons why Christians believe this.

First of all, on the night before he died, Jesus promised that he would send 'another' in his place (John 14:16). The clear implication of the Greek word that John uses here to describe the Holy Spirit (*parakletos*) is that he is 'another like Jesus'. This is personal language. It suggests that Jesus is promising the arrival of a person like himself but separate and distinct from him.

Secondly, when Jesus talked about the Holy Spirit he talked about a 'he', not an 'it'. Notice the following promise Jesus made, again during the evening before his death:

> *When the Spirit of truth comes, he will guide you into all truth. He will not speak on his own but will tell you what he has heard. He will tell you about the future. He will bring me glory by telling you whatever he receives from me.*
> John 16:13–14

These words are truly remarkable. Jesus uses the Greek word *pneuma* when he talks about the Spirit. This word is neuter, not masculine. Yet directly after using it, Jesus refers to this *pneuma* with the personal pronoun 'he'. This is grammatically strange. It is as if Jesus is deliberately stressing that the Spirit is not an impersonal force but a personal presence.

Thirdly, on a number of occasions in the New Testament the Spirit is spoken of as a person. Notice the following examples:

1. He teaches (John 14:26)
2. He guides (Acts 8:29)
3. He prays through us (Romans 8:26)
4. He can be grieved (Ephesians 4:30)
5. He can be lied to (Acts 5:3–4)
6. He can be resisted (Acts 7:51)

It is hard not to arrive at the conclusion that the New Testament speaks of the Holy Spirit in terms suggesting 'personhood'. The Holy Spirit is God's personal presence among and in believers.

The Holy Spirit is divine

The Holy Spirit is not only personal, he is divine. The things that are claimed about God in the Bible are also claimed about the Spirit. For example, one of the attributes of God we looked at in Chapter 2 was God's omnipresence – God is present everywhere in creation. What is claimed about God is also claimed about the Holy Spirit. So, in Psalm 139:7–10 we read:

> *I can never escape from your spirit!*
> *I can never get away from your presence!*
> *If I go up to heaven, you are there;*
> *if I go down to the grave, you are there.*
> *If I ride the wings of the morning,*
> *if I dwell by the farthest oceans,*
> *even there your hand will guide me,*
> *and your strength will support me.*

These beautiful words prove that the Holy Spirit is omnipresent, just as God is omnipresent. As Rodman Williams writes: 'The Holy Spirit is God. Whatever the various names or whatever the titles or symbols, all refer to God himself. The Holy Spirit is not some reality less than God: he is God.'

For this reason the Bible is not diffident in stating that the Holy Spirit has the attributes of God. The Holy Spirit gives life to all things, just as God does (Psalm 104:30). The Holy Spirit raises the dead, just as God does (Romans 8:11). He is eternal, just as God is (Hebrews 9:14). He is omniscient or 'all-knowing', just as God is (1 Corinthians 2:10). All this demonstrates that the Holy Spirit is divine. Jesus said 'God is Spirit' (John 4:24); the Spirit is also God. This is why Paul can say, 'the Lord is the Spirit' (2 Corinthians 3:17).

The Holy Spirit is accordingly the third person of the Godhead. He is a distinct, divine person. As the early church theologian Gregory of Nazianzus once wrote:

'What great things are there in the character of God which are not found in the Spirit? What titles which belong to God are not also applied to Him? He is called the Spirit of God, the Spirit of Christ, the mind of Christ, the Spirit of the Lord, the Spirit of adoption, of truth, of liberty; the Spirit of wisdom, of understanding, of counsel, of might, of knowledge, of godliness, of the fear of God. This only begins to show how unlimited He is.'

'The Holy Spirit is no less and no other than God himself, distinct from Him whom Jesus calls Father, distinct also from Jesus himself, yet no less than the Father and no less than Jesus, God Himself, God altogether.'

Karl Barth

The Holy Spirit is uncontainable

The Holy Spirit cannot be tied down or limited to one definition. For this reason the Bible uses many different images to describe the Holy Spirit.

He is described using the image of wind. In the Old Testament, the Hebrew word translated Spirit can also be translated wind (*ruach*). In the New Testament, the same is true of the Greek word *pneuma*. When the Holy Spirit comes upon the disciples in Acts 2 Luke says there was a sound like 'a mighty windstorm'. Jesus said this in John 3:8: 'Just as you can hear the wind but can't tell where

it comes from or where it is going, so you can't explain how people are born of the Spirit.' Like the wind, the Holy Spirit cannot be controlled.

The Holy Spirit is likened to fire in the Bible. John the Baptist promised that the Messiah (in other words, Jesus) would come and baptize people with the Holy Spirit and with fire. In Acts 2 the Spirit comes upon the disciples at Pentecost with 'what looked like flames or tongues of fire'. Fire speaks of cleansing and purifying.

The Holy Spirit is also compared to water. In John 7:37–38 Jesus said this: 'Anyone who is thirsty may come to me! Anyone who believes in me may come and drink! For the Scriptures declare "Rivers of living water will flow from his heart." The Gospel writer immediately afterwards explains that Jesus was speaking of the Spirit (verse 39).

So there are many images for the Holy Spirit. Others include oil, dove, guarantee, seal (as in a royal seal). These images are not to be used as proof that the Holy Spirit is impersonal (as, say, wind or fire is). Rather they are evidence of the uncontainable sovereignty of the Spirit of God. The great variety of these images points to the transcendent otherness of the Holy Spirit. He simply cannot be restricted to one simple definition.

The limitless nature of the Holy Spirit is further confirmed by the many different titles given to the Holy Spirit in the Bible. The following list is not exhaustive:

1. The Spirit of Truth (John 14:16-17)
2. The Spirit of Holiness (Romans 1:4)
3. The Spirit of Life (Romans 8:2)
4. The Spirit of Adoption (Romans 8:15)
5. The Spirit of Grace (Hebrews 10:29)
6. The Spirit of Glory (1 Peter 4:14)
7. The Spirit of God (Romans 8:9)

The Holy Spirit is the unlimited, personal presence of the living God. We can never say everything there is to say about him.

The Holy Spirit is revelatory

A fourth thing that is said about the Holy Spirit is that he brings the revelation of God to human beings. The apostle Peter tells us this about the Old Testament prophets in 2 Peter 1:20–21:

> *You must realize that no prophecy in Scripture ever came from the prophet's own understanding, or from human initiative. No, those prophets were moved by the Holy Spirit, and they spoke from God.*

Here Peter uses a particular metaphor to describe the inspiration of the prophets. He says they were 'carried along' by the Spirit. The picture is of ships with their sails being filled by strong winds and moved by their power.

In 1 Corinthians 2:11–12 Paul says this:

> *No one can know a person's thoughts except that person's own spirit, and no one can know God's thoughts except God's own Spirit. And we have received God's Spirit (not the world's spirit) so we can know the wonderful things God has freely given us.*

The Bible teaches that it is impossible to believe or understand who Jesus is or what Jesus came to do unless one has the Holy Spirit. The Holy Spirit brings revelation of Jesus to people's hearts. This is because the Holy Spirit's ministry is to make Jesus known and to reveal how great Jesus is. The Spirit is constantly pointing away from himself to Jesus, the Son of God. Canadian theologian James Packer describes this as the Spirit's 'floodlight' ministry. A building illuminated by hidden floodlights is a compelling image of how the Spirit works. The Spirit's work is not to draw attention to himself but to shine the light on Jesus so that people come to believe that Jesus is God's Son.

This aspect of the Holy Spirit's work cannot be understated. The thing that distinguishes the work of the Holy Spirit from all other spiritual experiences is this: the Holy Spirit glorifies Jesus. As the Puritan pastor Jonathan Edwards said in 1741, the primary characteristic of a genuine work of the Spirit is that it causes Jesus Christ to be honoured: 'When the operation is such as to raise their esteem of that Jesus who was born of the Virgin, and was crucified without the gates of Jerusalem; and seems more to confirm and establish their minds in the truth of what the gospel declares to us of his being the Son of God, and the Saviour of men; it is a sure sign that it is from the Spirit of God.' The Holy Spirit points to the real Jesus revealed in the New Testament.

And it is by this same Holy Spirit that a person comes to believe in Jesus and becomes a follower of Jesus. The Holy Spirit therefore not only enables people to receive revelation, he also enables them to receive salvation. While the work of Christ is a finished and objective fact, the benefits of this work still need to be appropriated in an individual's subjective experience. How then does that happen?

The answer given in the New Testament is 'by the Holy Spirit'. It is by the Holy Spirit that a person sees who Jesus really was and is and confesses him as Saviour and Lord (1 Corinthians 12:3). It is by the Holy Spirit that a person is convicted of their sins and repents in godly sorrow for all their past wrongdoing (John 16:8–11). It is by the Holy Spirit that a person begins life all over again in the experience of spiritual rebirth (John 3:3–5). It is by the Holy Spirit that a person is incorporated into the Son's intimate relationship with the Father, enabling them to call God 'Dearest Father' (Romans 8:15). The Holy Spirit is therefore indispensable for revelation and for salvation. Christians believe they cannot do without the Holy Spirit.

The Holy Spirit is powerful

An English lord was considering how to harness the power of the Niagara Falls. On one of his first visits he was told by his guide, 'This is the most powerful, untapped source of energy in

the universe.' The English lord replied, 'No, the Holy Spirit is the most powerful untapped source of energy in the universe.'

Christians believe that the Holy Spirit is the powerful presence of the living God. The power of the Holy Spirit is constantly illustrated throughout the pages of the Bible. In the Old Testament, the Holy Spirit comes upon special individuals in order to empower them for tasks. These moments of empowering are temporary, not permanent, and they are given to particular individuals, not to all God's people.

In the 400-year gap between the end of the last book of the Old Testament (Malachi) and the beginning of the New Testament (Matthew), the empowering presence of the Holy Spirit is noticeable for its absence. Jewish people of the day felt that the glory of God's presence had departed with the last of the prophets like Malachi. They were longing for the coming of the Messiah. They felt that the Messiah would usher in a new age of the Holy Spirit.

In the New Testament, Jesus is the fulfilment of these expectations. Jesus is himself empowered by the Holy Spirit at every point. He is conceived by the Holy Spirit (Luke 1:35). He is baptized in the Holy Spirit (Mark 1:9–11). His ministry of preaching the gospel, healing the sick and setting the captives free is all done in the power of the Holy Spirit (Luke 4:18–20). He suffers and dies, not in his strength alone, but with the help of the Holy Spirit (Hebrews 9:13). His resurrection from the dead is said to have been an act performed by the Holy Spirit (Romans 1:4). Everything about Jesus' life is Spirit-empowered.

> 'The Spirit-filled life is not a special deluxe edition of Christianity. It is part and parcel of the total plan of God for his people.'
> A. W. Tozer

With Jesus, the long drought of the Holy Spirit comes to an end and the new age of the Spirit begins. With Jesus, the empowering of the Holy Spirit is now permanent, not temporary, and it is for everyone who believes, not just a select few.

Jesus promises his disciples that he will baptize or drench them in the Holy Spirit and that is what he does on the day of Pentecost. God pours out his Spirit on the disciples, enabling them to speak to the nations with great courage about the wonders of God. As these early followers do this, they are not only enabled to speak boldly about Jesus (in the face of considerable opposition), they are also empowered to do great miracles. With the Spirit's help, they heal the sick, they bring freedom to the demonized, and they even raise the dead. Truly, the Holy Spirit is extraordinarily powerful. Think of the Niagara Falls when you think of the Spirit!

The community of the Holy Spirit

And all this brings us finally to the church. Just the mention of the word 'church' is likely nowadays to turn people off very quickly. This is because the church today can often, tragically, be very different from the New Testament vision of what it was destined to be. In the New Testament the church is an exciting idea. The church is compared to Christ's body, his bride, a temple, a family, a vine, a people, a royal priesthood, an olive tree, a flock, and so on. In the New Testament the church is understood as a people filled with the empowering presence of God. As the apostle Paul puts it:

> *We who believe are carefully joined together, becoming a holy temple for the Lord. Through him you Gentiles are also joined together as part of this dwelling where God lives by his Spirit.*
> Ephesians 2:21–22

What does the church look like when it becomes the dwelling place of the Holy Spirit?

It is a community in which people confess Jesus as Lord and call God their loving Father (1 Corinthians 12:3).

It is a community in which people are so filled with God's love that they cannot stop singing praises to the Father and the Son in heartfelt ways (Ephesians 5:18–20).

Gifts of the Spirit in the New Testament

The Bible teaches that God gives one or more gifts to every Christian. These gifts are a manifestation of the power of the Holy Spirit in the believer, and they are given for the good of the church as a whole (1 Corinthians 12:7). Here is a list of the gifts that the Bible mentions.

I Corinthians 12:8–10	I Corinthians 12:29–30	Romans 12:6–8	Ephesians 4:11
Word of wisdom			
Word of knowledge			
Faith			
Gifts of healing	Healing		
Miracles	Miracles		
Prophecy	Prophecy	Prophecy	Prophets
Discernment of spirits	Discernment of spirits		
Tongues	Tongues		
Interpretation of tongues			
	Apostles		Apostles
	Teachers	Teaching	Teachers
	Helps		
	Administration		
		Serving	
		Encouraging	
		Giving	
		Leadership	
		Mercy	
			Evangelists
			Pastors

It is a community in which the Holy Spirit inspires people to find and express their God-given creativity – in music, painting, dance, poetry, and many other ways (Exodus 35:30–35).

It is a community in which the Bible is preached in a powerful and inspirational way and where God's people are hungry to study and learn from the Scriptures (Acts 2:42).

It is a community in which people recognize their weakness in knowing how to pray but find the Holy Spirit praying through them in the way that Jesus wants them to (Romans 8:26–27).

It is a community in which people constantly remember what Jesus did at the cross, celebrating together the Lord's Supper (or Holy Communion), sensing Christ's presence with them when they do (Acts 2:46).

It is a community in which people leave their old sinful lifestyles behind, put to death the self-rule that ruins human life and relationships, and start to behave like Jesus and live a holy and authentic lifestyle (Galatians 5:19–23).

> 'Every time we say, "I believe in the Holy Spirit," we mean that we believe that there is a living God able and willing to enter human personality and change it.'
>
> J. B. Phillips

It is a community in which dividing walls are broken down and people of every nation find an astounding unity in their love for Jesus and their experience of being the adopted children of the same glorious Father (Galatians 4:5–6).

It is a community in which people have been set free from a spirit of ownership and possessiveness and instead give generously to the work of God and to those in need (Acts 2:44–45).

It is a community in which people know and use their spiritual gifts – gifts such as mercy for the poor and healing for the sick (Romans 12:6–8).

It is a community emboldened by the Holy Spirit to share the good news about Jesus locally, regionally, nationally and globally (Matthew 28:18–20).

It is a community committed to serving its neighbourhood in practical ways, leading to favour from those who do not yet belong and to the transformation of society (Acts 2:47).

It is a community in which people are filled with a Spirit-inspired longing for the liberation of the world from its

The fruit of the Spirit (Galatians 5:22–23)

The fruit of the Spirit differs from the gifts of the Spirit. The gifts are resources given by the Holy Spirit for Christian service. The fruit of the Spirit represents character qualities that the Holy Spirit helps every Christian to cultivate. These are:

Love, joy, peace (in our relationship with God)

Patience, kindness, goodness (in our relationships with others)

Faithfulness, gentleness, self-control (in our relationship with ourselves)

The Roman Catholic Church speaks about twelve qualities – the nine above plus generosity, chastity and modesty.

appalling pain – a groan that is shared by the universe itself (Romans 8:18–25).

It is a community in which everyone looks forward with hope to the return of Jesus, actively seeking to build the kingdom of heaven on earth as they wait.

Sounds exciting, doesn't it?

When the Holy Spirit is welcome in the church, the church becomes a community in which God's future is experienced in our today. In other words, the Christian community – when it is functioning in the way the New Testament envisages – becomes a foretaste of heaven on earth. The Holy Spirit is the power of the age to come. When he is welcomed in the church, the church becomes an antidote to the chill of despair in the world and becomes a place of overflowing hope.

9 Last Things

On 11 September 2001, a Christian called Todd Beamer died when his aeroplane, flight 93, was hijacked and crashed into a field in Pennsylvania. A year later his widow Lisa (also a Christian) was interviewed. She made this remarkable statement: 'Personally, I'm less afraid now than I was before September 11 because I have a greater sense of God's sovereignty. He's in control, and he has a plan for the world. Not only that, he has plans for me individually. And he loves me more than any human being ever could love me. So what's really to fear?'

> 'We have one life; it soon will be past; what we do for God is all that will last.'
> Muhammed Ali

What is it that gives Christians this distinctive ability to see past today's pain to tomorrow's promise? The answer is 'hope'. Christians are supremely people of hope. This is not idealistic hope, a hope that denies the existence of suffering, pretending that it is not there. Christian hope is what G. K. Chesterton described as a sense of expectancy when things are otherwise hopeless. Christians believe that history is not an endless repetition of cycles but rather a story authored by God with a beginning, a middle and an end. Christians believe that God has a plan for his creation and that everything is heading towards a divinely ordained goal when suffering will come to an end and evil will be defeated. As we read in Ephesians:

> God's secret plan has now been revealed to us; it is a plan centered on Christ, designed long ago according to his good pleasure. And this is his plan: At the right time he will bring everything together under the authority of Christ — everything in heaven and on earth.
> Ephesians 1:9–10

In this final chapter we will see that the source of this hope is in the teaching of Jesus and in the promises of God revealed in the Bible. In other words, the grounds of Christian hope are not the quicksand of shallow Utopianism but the solid rock of God's special revelation (see Chapter 1). God's special revelation shows us the end game for human history. Reading the end of God's book, the Bible, we know in advance how it is all going to end – and it's all going to end with Jesus.

The future kingdom

The Jewish people at the time of Jesus believed that history had a purpose and that one day God would intervene to save his people and to judge the world. This day of intervention was expected in the long-term future. On that day, God's kingdom would be established in Israel and God's reign would be extended throughout the world.

When Jesus started teaching nearly 2,000 years ago he made a very radical, startling and dramatic claim. He told his contemporaries that this eagerly anticipated kingdom had arrived already and that it had come in his own ministry. He was not saying by this that the end of the world had come. What he was saying was that the things expected at the end of history – such as God forgiving sins and raising the dead – were happening in advance in his ministry.

This is why we find Jesus speaking so much about God's rule at the end of time as a present reality. In Jesus' teaching the kingdom of God is an 'inaugurated' kingdom. It has come now. So we read in Mark's Gospel:

> Later on, after John was arrested by Herod Antipas, Jesus went to Galilee to preach God's good news. 'At last the time has come!' he announced. 'The kingdom of God is near! Turn from your sins and believe this good news!'
> Mark 1:14–15

At the same time, Jesus not only teaches that the kingdom has come. He also teaches that the fullness of this kingdom will not be seen on the earth until God decides that the last day of history has arrived. So there is much in Jesus' teaching that sounds 'apocalyptic'; in other words, Jesus unveils the secret

facts of the end of history to his disciples. For example, towards
the end of Mark's Gospel, Jesus describes the unfolding drama
that will attend the final events of history:

> *At that time, after those horrible days end,*
> *the sun will be darkened,*
> *the moon will not give light,*
> *the stars will fall from the sky,*
> *and the powers of heaven will be shaken.*
>
> *Then everyone will see the Son of Man arrive on the clouds with great*
> *power and glory. And he will send forth his angels to gather together his*
> *chosen ones from all over the world – from the farthest ends of the earth*
> *and heaven.*

Mark 13:24–27

Christians are often required to hold two apparently opposing views in tension at the same time. This is called 'embracing paradox'. Jesus' teaching on the kingdom of God is no exception. He can say that 'the kingdom has arrived' (Matthew 12:28) and at the same time tell his disciples to pray to God, 'Your kingdom come' (Matthew 6:10). The end has already arrived in Jesus' ministry, but at the same time it is yet to come fully. It is both already and not yet.

The final facts

One of my favourite TV programmes when I was a boy was *The A-Team*. Every episode followed a similar pattern with the members of the A-Team devising plans to rescue others and sometimes themselves. The end of each episode usually had the catch phrase, 'Don't you just love it when a plan comes together?'

The Bible reveals that God has a plan to rescue his creation and that this plan is coming together. This plan has already come into effect with the first coming of Jesus Christ. But the Bible promises that there will be a second coming of Christ at the end of history. When that happens, the final act of rescue will occur and evil will be totally and irrevocably eradicated from the world.

'The purpose of life is to find out who am I? Why am I here? Where am I going? That's what we need answering.'

George Harrison

Christians hold some important beliefs about the fulfilment of God's plan for the end of time. This branch of Christian belief is often known as 'eschatology', from the Greek words *eschata* meaning 'last things' and *logos* meaning speech. Eschatology is speaking about the last things or the final facts of history. The four last things that this subject deals with are:

• The return of Jesus Christ

• The resurrection of the dead

• The last judgment

• Heaven and hell

In what follows we will look at each of these final facts.

121

The return of Jesus Christ

Christians don't tend to say, 'Look what the world is coming to.' They are more likely to say, 'Look what's coming to the world.' What's coming to the world is Jesus Christ. When Jesus left the disciples at the ascension the angels said to them, 'Men of Galilee, why are you standing here staring at the sky? Jesus has been taken away from you into heaven. And someday, just as you saw him go, he will return!' (Acts 1:11). Jesus is coming back to the world. That is at the very heart of the Christian's hope.

In the 260 chapters of the New Testament there are 318 references to the return of Jesus Christ at the end of history. Some twentieth-century Christians have argued that the second coming of Jesus is a myth. They have proposed that Jesus is not coming again on some future date in history, saying that this is picture language. It is a symbolic way of describing an experience of Jesus 'coming to me' in a climactic way in my own personal history.

While some Christians believe this, most reject a purely existentialist interpretation of the return of Christ and argue that the Bible is describing future *facts* (albeit using a lot of

Entrance of Charles VIII into Naples, *12 May 1495. An anonymous nineteenth-century painting from the Palace of Versailles.*

symbolic language). The most common word used by the New Testament writers to describe Christ's return is the Greek word *parousia*. In the ancient world, *parousia* was used to describe the sudden arrival of a ruler. This is the word the apostle Paul uses in 1 Thessalonians 4:15–18:

> *I can tell you this directly from the Lord: We who are still living when the Lord returns [parousia] will not rise to meet him ahead of those who are in their graves. For the Lord himself will come down from heaven with a commanding shout, with the call of the archangel, and with the trumpet call of God. First, all the Christians who have died will rise from their graves. Then, together with them, we who are still alive and remain on the earth will be caught up in the clouds to meet the Lord in the air and remain with him forever.*

The second coming of Jesus Christ is supremely a *parousia* – the sudden arrival not of a mere earthly ruler but of the King of kings. It is spoken about in the New Testament as a future event, not as a symbolic way of describing a present reality. As we read in Hebrews 9:28, 'He will come again but not to deal with our sins again. This time he will bring salvation to all those who are eagerly waiting for him.' Belief in Christ's return at the end of history is central to orthodox Christian faith.

When will this event happen? The Bible does not give us a specific date. Although Jesus describes the kinds of signs that will precede and accompany his return (see Mark 13), he also warns against trying to speculate when the exact time will be. In Acts 1:7, Jesus tells his disciples that 'the Father sets those dates and they are not for you to know'. Some Christians spend a lot of time trying to anticipate the date of the *parousia*. This mostly happens in sectarian groups. But as G. K. Chesterton once remarked, when such sects talk about the end of the world, it is the sect that ends, not the world! Dating the return of Christ is therefore foolish. As someone once said, Christians are to be on the welcoming committee not the planning committee.

Christians therefore believe that Jesus Christ will return on the last day of history. There are some who doubt this on the grounds that the New Testament speaks of this event as very imminent. This issue of the delay of the *parousia* has been greatly exaggerated. There are only a few obvious references to this sense of imminent return (see Romans 13:11–12, 1 Corinthians 7:29, 1 Peter 4:7). Jesus teaches that the future date of the second coming is unknown (Mark 13:32).

The resurrection of the dead

Dr Timothy LaHaye is one of the most successful novelists in the world today. He has written a whole series about the end of the world from a Christian perspective. Millions of people have read these books, most of which have the tag line of the first novel, *Left Behind*.

While these novels have been very popular, they have not been without controversy. This is because the author holds a specific set of beliefs about the final facts of history. One of these is that in the passage quoted above (from 1 Thessalonians 4:15–18) the apostle Paul is referring to an event known as 'the rapture'. This says that when history is about to close, Jesus will 'rapture' or 'seize' his people from the earth and gather them to himself. Christians will leave everyone else behind to face a time of great difficulty on the earth known as the 'great tribulation'. LaHaye's novels promote this belief – a belief known as 'the pre-tribulation rapture'. However, not all Christians agree about the fact, nature and timing of this 'rapture'. The novels have therefore not been without their critics.

One thing that all Christians agree on is that when Christ returns there will be what is known as 'the general resurrection'. All those who have died will be resurrected on the last day of history. This is the second of the final facts, after the fact of Christ's return.

It is really important to note that the Bible does not teach that human beings are naturally immortal. It nowhere says that we have immortal souls – as some of the ancient Greek philosophers believed. Rather, in the Bible, only God is described as immortal (1 Timothy 6:16). We are not.

If we are not naturally immortal, how then can we live forever in heaven? Christians believe that immortality is something that God will confer to everyone at the general resurrection. This doesn't mean that everyone will live forever in the presence of God in heaven. This idea (known as universalism) is not a mainstream Christian belief. It does mean that God plans to raise every human being from the dead on the day of his Son's return and that this will be a bodily and an immortal resurrection.

When we look at the Bible's teaching on the general resurrection of the dead it becomes clear that God's plan is to raise Christians first. Paul says in 1 Corinthians 15:23, 'There is an order to this resurrection: Christ was raised first; then when Christ comes back, all his people will be raised.' When Christians are raised, immortality will be given to them as a divine gift. As Paul says in 1 Corinthians 15:42, 'Our earthly bodies, which die and decay, will be different when they are resurrected, for they will never die.' He goes on to add

The rapture

The word *rapture* – which is not found in the Bible – is a transliteration of the old Latin word *rapere*, which means to 'seize' or 'snatch away'. In 1 Thessalonians 4:17, the apostle Paul says that Jesus Christ will one day come back and Christians (whether alive or dead) will be caught up to meet him in the air. Some Christians believe that this meeting in the air will occur after Christians have been 'raptured'. They say that this will all happen in the twinkling of an eye and it will involve the bodies of Christian people being instantly transformed into resurrected bodies (1 Corinthians 15:51–52). The biggest question, aside from whether the Bible actually teaches 'the rapture', concerns when this event will occur in relation to what is called the 'great tribulation' – the time of great cosmic and global suffering prophesied by Jesus in Matthew 24. Some say before, others during, and still others after. There is much debate about these issues, especially in North America. The most popular view (supported by novelist Timothy LaHaye) is that Christians will be snatched away before the great tribulation. It should be noted that neither the Roman Catholic nor the Orthodox Church teaches this doctrine.

these thoughts about the 'glorification' of believers:

> *When the trumpet sounds, the Christians who have died will be raised with transformed bodies. And then we who are living will be transformed so that we will never die. For our perishable earthly bodies must be transformed into heavenly bodies that will never die.*
> 1 Corinthians 15:52–53

Having read this, some are likely to ask two questions. The first is this: What happens to everyone else (in other words, those who are not Christians) when they are resurrected? The second is: What happens to people between their death and their resurrection?

The Chosen and the Resurrection of the Dead, *sculpture by Lorenzo Maitani (thirteenth to fourteenth century) in Orvieto Cathedral.*

What then of the future resurrection of non-Christians? What will happen to those who have rejected God in this life? The Bible is quite clear on this: they too will be raised in an immortal state when Christ returns. However, we will see in a few moments that there are quite different destinies for those who have forsaken God and those who have believed in God. This will bring us to the matter of heaven and hell – a much neglected subject in today's world.

What happens to people between their death and resurrection?

When a Christian dies, their soul or spirit goes in a disembodied state to be with Jesus. This is the meaning of Paul's teaching in 2 Corinthians 5:1–18. In this disembodied state, the Christian passes beyond the constraints of time and space. Here there is no consciousness of time passing. Some Christians believe that this means being in a state of what is called 'soul sleep' (a belief known as 'psychopannychism'). Others contend that immediately after death believers are 'with the Lord' in a conscious rather than an unconscious state (Luke 23:43; 2 Corinthians 5:8). There they remain until the general resurrection when their souls are reunited with their newly resurrected bodies. Still others believe that Christians go to purgatory – a place where imperfect souls are prepared through painful refining for heaven; however, this belief is hard to square with what the Bible teaches and Jesus nowhere mentions it.

What about those who have not been followers of Jesus Christ? What happens to them?

Here we are on less certain ground. It seems from Scripture that when a non-Christian dies their soul or spirit goes in a disembodied state to a place where Jesus is not present. This is the realm of the dead, a place of darkness and shadows. In the Greek New Testament the word used to refer to this place is 'Hades' (Acts 2:27). In the Hebrew Old Testament the word is 'Sheol'. These words refer to the intermediate state for those who do not follow Jesus Christ in their earthly lives. When Jesus Christ returns, those consigned to the realm of the dead will be reunited with their resurrected bodies, in preparation for judgment.

The last judgment

While every human being will become immortal at the return of Christ (with the general resurrection), not all will be for ever in heaven with the Father. Though it is currently not a popular thing to say, orthodox Christian belief states that human beings live in a moral universe, that we are all accountable for our actions, and that one day there will be a final reckoning before God. This reckoning is known as the last judgment.

The belief in the last judgment is a very important one, especially for those who have been the victims of injustice. For them, the idea of a final settling of accounts is extremely important, not least in terms of how they view God. As theologian Jim Packer puts it, 'Would a God who did not care about the difference between right and wrong be a good and admirable being? Would a God who put no distinction between the beasts of history (Hitler and Stalin, for example) and his own saints be morally praiseworthy and perfect?' The answer is clearly no. An indifference to such moral questions would evidently make God imperfect not perfect, uncaring not loving. The proof that God is both perfect and loving is the fact that he has committed himself in the Bible to a final judgment upon the world.

Christians accordingly believe that there will be a last judgment. This belief holds that Jesus will be the judge (Acts 10:42). On that day there will be a separation of the good and the evil. As Jesus said in Matthew's Gospel:

> When the Son of Man comes in his glory, and all the angels with him, then he will sit upon his glorious throne. All the nations will be gathered in his presence, and he will separate them as a shepherd separates the sheep from the goats.
> Matthew 25:31–32

On this day, everyone who has ever lived will be judged by Jesus. Paul describes this event in 2 Thessalonians 1:8–9: 'He will

come with his mighty angels, in flaming fire, bringing judgment on those who don't know God and on those who refuse to obey the Good News of our Lord Jesus. They will be punished with everlasting destruction, forever separated from the Lord.' On the day of judgment there will be a great polarization. On one side there will be those who didn't know God and rejected the good news about Jesus. On the other will be those who did know God and those who accepted the gospel, the good news about Jesus. Many Christians also believe that there will be people on this side who never heard the gospel but who responded to what God was saying to them through their consciences, through creation and so forth (see Acts 17:27–31 and Chapter 1 on general revelation).

Fresco painting of the Last Judgment by Giorgio Vasari, painted between 1572 and 1579 inside the dome of the Duomo Santa Maria del Fiore, Florence, Italy.

> 'When the author walks onto the stage, the play is over. God is going to invade, all right; but what is the good of saying you are on His side then, when you see the whole natural universe melting away like a dream and something else comes crashing in? This time it will be God without disguise; something so overwhelming that it will strike either irresistible love or irresistible horror into every creature. It will be too late then to choose your side. That will not be the time for choosing; it will be the time when we discover which side we really have chosen, whether we realized it before or not. Now, today, this moment, is our chance to choose the right side.'
>
> C. S. Lewis.

Will Christians also be judged? The answer is yes. The Bible says that we will all stand before the judgment seat of God (Romans 14:10, 12). This is not to say that Christians will be condemned to eternal punishment. The Bible makes it clear that there is no condemnation for those who are in Christ Jesus (Romans 8:1) so Christians are not to be fearful (1 John 4:18). What it does mean is that God expects the faith of a Christian to be active, not passive. While Christians cannot be saved by good works, they are expected to do good works once they are saved. Those believers who serve God faithfully will have heavenly rewards (2 Corinthians 5:10; Luke 19:17, 19). Those who don't will still be saved, but like people escaping through a wall of flames (1 Corinthians 3:15). They will still experience the everlasting joy of heaven, but they will miss out on the rewards for faithfulness and holiness while they lived on earth. It is for this reason that the New Testament writers constantly emphasize the importance of living a holy life and finishing well.

Heaven and hell

Christians believe that Christ is returning on the last day of history and that there will be a final judgment. They also believe that this judgment will determine which of two eternal destinies every human being will receive. The first is heaven. The second is hell.

Let's deal with the bad news first.

According to the New Testament, hell is a place reserved for the wicked. Fewer and fewer Christians talk about this today. Many deny that a good God could consign even the worst of people to hell. A.W. Tozer pointed to this when he wrote that 'the vague and tenuous hope that God is too kind to punish the ungodly has become a deadly opiate for the consciences of millions'. Jesus however did not shrink from talking about hell.

The word translated 'hell' in the Greek New Testament is *Gehenna* (*Gehinnom* in Hebrew). This was a rubbish dump outside the walls of Jerusalem where all the city refuse was taken to be burned. It was a place frequented by dogs and wild animals who gnawed away at the remains of executed

criminals and decaying food. Originally it had been a place where children had been sacrificed (2 Chronicles 28:3). It was therefore in Jewish thought a place associated with God's utter condemnation of sin. When Jesus talked about hell it was as if he was saying, 'If you want to know what an eternity without God is like, go to the rubbish dump outside Jerusalem, where there's fire burning day and night, and where the sound of gnashing teeth can be heard from the walls.' Jesus assumed the existence of hell. He didn't argue for its existence.

In Jesus' teaching, hell is portrayed as a place of fire (Matthew 5:22) and a place of darkness (Matthew 8:12). Jesus warned his hearers that hell existed. He also warned evildoers that if they did not repent and change their ways they would be like the following:

- Incinerated chaff (Matthew 3:12)

- Weeds pulled up and burnt (Matthew 13:40)

- A tree cut down and burnt (Matthew 7:19)

- An uprooted plant (Matthew 15:13)

- Bad fish thrown away (Matthew 13:48)

- A house that falls down (Matthew 7:27)

- Wicked tenants punished (Matthew 21:41)

- The crushing of a person under a mighty stone (Matthew 21:44)

- An evil servant cut to pieces (Matthew 24:51)

- A debtor imprisoned (Matthew 18:34)

- A party-goer ejected into outer darkness (Matthew 22:13)

- A worthless servant thrown into outer darkness (Matthew 25:30)

Just how literally we are meant to take this language is debatable. In the Middle Ages Christian teachers interpreted such imagery literally and even developed more lurid descriptions of hell in order to create a climate of fear. Today Christians are less likely to interpret such language absolutely literally and are more inclined to see it as symbolic of the ultimate nightmare – exclusion for ever from God's presence.

In addition to this, there has been a debate among Christians concerning the idea of 'eternal' punishment. Some believe that evildoers, having been resurrected in an immortal state, will suffer eternally and consciously the consequences of their decision-making in this life. Others, known as *annihilationists*, believe that the wicked will be extinguished for ever. They do not agree that 'eternal punishment' means 'punishment consciously experienced for ever', but rather 'the punishment of being annihilated for ever'.

These debates will no doubt continue. Whatever the outcome, conventional Christian belief says that hell exists. More than that, mainstream or orthodox Christians will contend that the church must not neglect this topic. As the one-time American politician Charles Colson puts it:

'When the church does not clearly teach the doctrine of hell, society loses an important anchor. In a sense, hell gives meaning to our lives. It tells us that the moral choices we make day by day have eternal significance; that our behaviour has consequences lasting to eternity; that God Himself takes our choices seriously. When people don't believe in a final judgment, they don't feel ultimately accountable for their actions. There is no firm leash holding back sinful impulses.'

All this is bad news. But there is good news too. The Bible speaks of another destiny besides hell, and this is heaven. If hell ultimately means eternal exclusion from the presence of God, heaven means eternal inclusion in God's presence. Heaven is not described in great detail in the Bible. The most important thing to say about it is that heaven is where Jesus is. It is living for ever with him.

The New Testament tells us that there is going to be a new

heaven and a new earth. Revelation 21:1–2 says:

> *Then I saw a new heaven and a new earth, for the old heaven and the old earth had disappeared. And the sea was also gone. And I saw the holy city, the new Jerusalem, coming down from God out of heaven like a beautiful bride prepared for her husband.*

This new heaven and new earth will be formed out of the existing heaven and earth. The Bible speaks of a great purging of the existing cosmos by fire. After that, the holy city (which Jesus has been preparing since the time of his ascension) will come down to this renovated universe. This city will be where God dwells with his people (Hebrews 11:10). It will be a city without a cemetery because there will be no more dying. As it says in Revelation 21:3–4:

> *God himself will be with them. He will remove all of their sorrows, and there will be no more death or sorrow or crying or pain. For the old world and its evils are gone forever.*

Christians believe in the reality of heaven. However, they do not believe that they are going 'up to heaven'. The traditional language of 'going to heaven when I die' is completely misleading. It is more accurate to say that heaven is coming to where God's people are when Jesus comes back. One day God is going to make all things new. The best is yet to be, not only for individual Christians, but for the whole of creation.

> '**When you were born, you cried and the world rejoiced. Live your life in a manner so that when you die the world cries and you rejoice.**'
>
> Native American proverb

One thing is for sure: God's goal is heaven. God has been preparing a heavenly kingdom for his people since the foundation of the world (Matthew 25:34). God has also created a place known as 'hell', but hell is primarily prepared as a place for the devil and his angels (Matthew 25:43). If human beings go there it is because they have consciously chosen in this life to live outside God's presence, without reference to God. Those who choose to forsake God in this life will experience the fullness of what it means to be God-forsaken in eternity. Those who choose to live for God in this life will enjoy him for ever. For Christians, heaven is home.

So 'heaven' is a reality, and the offer is open for everyone to make heaven their home, in this life and in the life to come. All a person needs to do to enter the kingdom of heaven is to repent of past sin and to receive God's forgiveness, available to all. In addition a person needs to go on putting their faith and trust in Jesus for the whole of their lives, knowing that this friendship lasts for eternity, not just for now.

> **Millennium**
>
> Millennialism comes from the word 'millennium', which literally means 'one thousand years'. It is a belief embraced by some Christians that there will be a 1,000-year golden age in which Jesus Christ will reign on the earth prior to the final judgment. It is primarily derived from Revelation 20:1–6 and is usually referred to as 'premillennialism'.

Living with hope

Christians are people who not only enjoy forgiveness for the past and new life in the present. They also live with a great hope for the future. This hope is one that looks past the world's present suffering to that point when Jesus Christ will return, when the dead will be raised, when every human being will be judged, and when the good will be rewarded and the wicked punished. All this suggests a future eagerly to be expected. Indeed Christians are not so much citizens of this earth making their way to heaven; they are citizens of heaven making their way through this earth.

This should not imply for one moment that Christians are so fixated on the future that they do nothing to alleviate the sufferings of the present. That is in fact not true at all. It was C. S. Lewis who said that it has been those who have believed most in heaven who have done most to improve people's lot in this life. Take the great social reformer William Wilberforce as an example.

This is in fact where the language of 'heaven up there' (in some spatial sense) is unhelpful. Jesus talked a lot about the kingdom of heaven. In that teaching he emphasized that this

> '...there is more joy in heaven over one lost sinner who repents and returns to God than over ninety-nine others who are righteous and haven't strayed away!'
> Luke 15:7

heavenly kingdom was meant to be here where we are. As Bono of U2 has recently said:

> I close my eyes and I try to imagine heaven… but I think heaven is on earth. That's my prayer. It was Christ's prayer. It was Christ's prayer which was 'Thy kingdom come, thy will be done, on earth as it is in heaven'… We've got to start bringing heaven down to earth now. So what I imagine heaven looks like is this present life without this present evil…

While the last words of the Bible are 'Come, Lord Jesus', this hope for the future does not mean that Christians should desire to escape from this present world. Rather, it means that Christians want to work hard with the help of the Holy Spirit to help those who are experiencing hell on earth to experience a foretaste of heaven right now.

And that is something worth working towards.

Index

Page numbers shown in bold
indicate a main entry.

F

G

H

M

Mary Magdalene 94–95, 99
Mary, mother of Jesus 7, 63,
  66–68, 75
Mass 88–89
Mercy 26, 115, 116
Messiah 97, 110, 113
Millennialism 135
Miracles 63, 106, 114, 115
Monism 44
Monotheism 70
Morality 12, **24–25**, 48
Mystery **9–10**, 32, 74
Myth 16, 47, 55, 59, 74, 100, 122

N

Natural Theology 14, 23
Naturalism 100
Nature 10, 12–13, 14
Nestorianism 72

O

Omnipotence 26
Omnipresence 26, 74, 108
Omniscience 26
Original Sin **50–51**, 56, 57, 59
Orthodox Church 16, 56, 125

P

Parousia 123–24
Passion of Christ 75–77

Pelagius 56, 79
Pentecost 86, **104–106**, 110, 114
Pentecostalism 106
Personhood of the Holy Spirit 108
Pneuma 107, 109
Pre-millennialism 135
Process Theology
Prophecy 33
Prophets 16, 111, 113
Protestantism 67, 89
Providence 32
Psychopannychism 127

R

Ransom 77, 82
Rapture 124–25
Rationality 48, 60
Reason **21–22**, 24–25, 27, 46, 48
Recapitulation 77
Reconciliation 55, **85**, 88
Redemption 81–82
Repentance 79, 83, 90, 112, 135
Resurrection
  Final 125, 128
  Of Jesus 69, 86, 91–117
  Of the body 8, 125, 127
Revelation **9–20**, 24–25, 29, 30,
  34, 41, 111, 112, 119
Reward 79, 130, 135
Roman Catholic Church 16, 67,
  89, 117, 125
Ruach 109

S

Sabbath 43, 64, 96
Sacrifice 82–84

Picture Acknowledgments

p. 6 Digital Art/CORBIS; pp. 8–9 Guy Edwardes/Getty Images Ltd; p. 11 Digital Vision/Getty Images Ltd; p. 14 Channel Island Pictures/Alamy; p. 18 Andy Rous; p. 22 Andy Rous; p. 23 Lion Hudson Plc; p. 31 Andy Rous; p. 35 Ian McKinnell/Alamy; pp. 38–39 Cephas Picture Library/Alamy; p. 41 Preston Schlebusch/The Image Bank/Getty Images Ltd; p. 46 Visual Arts Library (London)/Alamy; p. 49 Harald Eisenberger/Getty Images Ltd; p. 50 Visual Arts Library (London)/Alamy; p. 52 The Bridgeman Art Library/Getty Images Ltd; p. 55 Adastra/Taxi/Getty Images Ltd; pp. 58–59 Alfio Scigliano/Sygma/Corbis; p. 62 Gianni Dagli Orti/Corbis; p. 67 Francis G. Mayer/Corbis; pp. 72–73 Nebbia, Cesare (1534–1614): Vatican Library © 1990. Photo Scala, Florence; p. 76 Antoine Gyori/Corbis Syma; p. 78 Glasgow City Council (Museums); p. 81 Bojan Brecelj/Corbis; p. 83 Hanan Isachar; p. 87 Ron Sachs/CNP/Corbis; p. 91 Lion Hudson Plc; pp. 96–97 Getty Images Ltd; p. 99 Arte & Immagini srl/CORBIS; p. 102 David Cavagnaro/ Visuals Unlimited/Getty Images Ltd; p. 105 The Art Archive/ Galleria Nazionale dell'Umbria Perugia/Dagli Orti; pp. 108–109 Phil Degginger/Alamy; p. 111 David Angel/ Alamy; p. 113 Nicholas Rous; p. 120 Dennis di Cicco/Corbis; p. 122 The Print Collector/Alamy; pp. 124–25 Maitani, Lorenxo (13th–14th century): Orvieto, Cathedral © 1990. Photo Scala, Florence; p. 129 M.Flynn/Alamy; p. 132–33 Les Stone/ZUMA/Corbis; pp. 136–37 Philip Nealey/Getty Images Ltd.